GUESTIQUETTE

GUESTIQUETTE

A Handbook for
Horrible Houseguests

TOM COLEMAN

Illustrations by Joe Stuart

Andrews McMeel
PUBLISHING®

Andrews McMeel Publishing
a division of Andrews McMeel Universal
1130 Walnut Street, Kansas City, Missouri 64106

www.andrewsmcmeel.com

24 25 26 27 28 SDB 10 9 8 7 6 5 4 3 2 1

ISBN: 978-1-5248-9006-3

Library of Congress Control Number: 2024931654

Editor: Betty Wong
Art Director: Holly Swayne
Production Editor: Brianna Westervelt
Production Manager: Tamara Haus

ATTENTION: SCHOOLS AND BUSINESSES
Andrews McMeel books are available at quantity discounts with bulk purchase for educational, business, or sales promotional use. For information, please e-mail the Andrews McMeel Publishing Special Sales Department: sales@amuniversal.com.

For my sister, Mary Joan

CONTENTS

Should we give them the "just here for one night"
olive oil, the "spending the weekend" candle or the
"not sure how long we're staying" coffee table book?

INTRODUCTION

Fun fact: Fergie (the Duchess of York, *not* the Black Eyed Pea) questioned whether this book should happen. You see, I got into a conversation with her at a recent Thanksgiving dinner, and somewhere between the oyster stuffing and the marshmallow sweet potatoes, she voiced her misgivings about an American (me) writing a book about etiquette. Realizing that someone *clearly* was still not over that nasty breakup of 1776, I tried to assure the doubtful duchess that *Guestiquette* is NOT an etiquette book. *Guestiquette* goes way beyond etiquette—and then a little further—offering practical advice to help navigate the surprisingly tricky world of being a houseguest. What is the protocol if you're a vegan houseguest in a home full of ferocious meat-eaters? How do you save face after getting overly frisky and breaking the guest room bed? Can you steal the hair dryer if you're invited to stay at the White House? Etiquette focuses on "polite" situations and things like how to write a thank-you note. *Guestiquette* realizes that "polite" isn't always possible and serves as a useful and honest guide for houseguest and host. (Spoiler: Emily Post never dealt with how to behave when you're a houseguest during a zombie apocalypse.)

In addition to advice, *Guestiquette* has charts, graphs, lists, and even a recipe that all celebrate the world of being a houseguest. You'll also find true first-person accounts from hosts and houseguests who were brave enough to share their harrowing and often cringe-inducing stories.

As we all begin to dip our toes back into the traveling pool post-pandemic and start visiting friends and family once again, don't be surprised if you're a little rusty in regard to houseguest conduct. It's been a minute since we dragged around our wheely luggage, so it's understandable if you need a little time to fully regain your houseguest sea legs. *Guestiquette* offers you a quick little refresher course. Not sure what to do if you find a dead mouse under your bed or feel guilty after leading that sangria-chugging contest at your host's dinner party? Fear not—*Guestiquette* has the answers for even the most horrible houseguest. As to why I'm qualified to write this book, please under no circumstances assume it's because I am the perfect houseguest. There are more than a few former hosts of mine who would do a spit take at the notion that I am an ideal guest. However, while I may never be in the Houseguest Hall of Fame, I have been a houseguest so often and in so many different situations that I recognize what constitutes horrible houseguest behavior and what you can do to avoid it. Oh, and if you're wondering why the hell I was having Thanksgiving dinner with Fergie . . . well, that's another book.

—Tom Coleman

OUR CAVE OR YOURS?
Guestiquette History

Somewhere in a tiny office with a jade plant on the windowsill, there is no doubt a tweedy historian who could educate us all on the origins of the houseguest. Doctoral dissertations may have been devoted to the topic, with titles like "If These Duvets Could Talk: An Exploration of the Houseguest through the Ages." Yet it's still impossible to pinpoint the world's very first houseguest. It's likely it was prehistoric man who first packed up a couple sharp rocks and an animal skin (in case it got chilly) and headed off to stay with others. Their visits were probably more about finding food and safety in numbers from things that could eat *them*, versus going to check out their host's new kitchen. Of course, circumstances back then were far different from today, but undoubtedly cave-dwelling hosts witnessed houseguest behavior they viewed as Neanderthal even for Neanderthals. "Do you believe he ate ALL the wooly mammoth?" Thus, the need for guestiquette was born.

As time marched on, there were new situations that could use some houseguest guidance. Ancient Greece introduced revolutionary thought in medicine, philosophy, and science. So imagine a host having to deal with a houseguest full of the grape who wouldn't shut up about his new "the earth is a globe" theory. Plus, what about the houseguests who expected their hosts to get them good seats at the Olympics? Boundaries were needed, people.

The Middle Ages brought about a whole new set of houseguest issues, the most pressing being a little something called the black plague. A houseguest who snores is one thing, but letting someone stay in your home who could wipe out the whole village—that was kind of a lot to ask.

These events may have provided a foundation for the "fake sick excuse," often utilized by the hosts of today. Next time you hear somone say "We'd love you to visit, but Brian has the flu and we wouldn't want you to catch it," remember that it can all be traced back to lice on rats.

The first evidence of guestiquette influence in America came with the arrival of the Pilgrims and the first Thanksgiving. Guests arriving later were relegated to the first-ever "kids' table," and feelings were hurt when, much like today, nobody would even *try* the cranberry sauce.

Proper guestiquette is needed now more than ever. Horrible house-guest behavior comes in many forms and can happen in every situation. You just need some guidance to avoid it, so that when your host tells you to "Come back anytime!" they actually mean it.

HOUSEGUEST
HALL OF FAME

King Lear
Harry Potter
Oliver Quick
Mary and Percy Shelley
Leon Black
Paul Sheldon
Brad and Janet
The Cat in the Hat
Tom Ripley
Julian Assange
Mork from Ork
John Wilkes Booth
Greg Focker
Paddington
Jonathan Harker
Mary and Joseph
E. T.
Kato Kaelin
The Fresh Prince of Bel-Air
Most characters in Jane Austen
Goldilocks

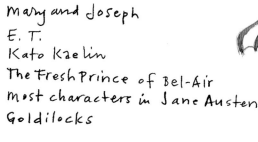

CHAPTER 1

URBAN PLANNING
The City Houseguest

So many cities, so many invitations . . . who cares if most were made when alcohol was involved? An invite IS an invite.

The first thing to remember as a city houseguest is that unlike you, your host is most likely not on holiday and is politely tolerating your presence in their home. It's not that they don't want you there; it's just that it disrupts their routine. They're going to work every day, and when they come home and turn that key, they know it's likely they'll find someone sitting on their sofa who isn't usually there. Someone who makes it impossible for them to instantly unwind and take off their pants the second they get through the door. *Never forget the sacrifices your host is making for you.*

Another thing to consider when a city guest is limited space. If you get your own room with an actual bed, you've hit the jackpot, but there's a good chance your accommodations could be a bit more "rough hewn." A couch, an air mattress, a race car bed in a playroom, these are all possibilities, and if offered, thank your host profusely without even the tiniest twitch of dissatisfaction.

If left alone while your host is at work, don't treat the place like your parents are away for the weekend. Don't crank your music, always wipe down the sink, and don't open new jars of anything. "Hey, would you mind if I opened that mustard you bought on your trip to Provence that you've been saving for three years?" *Of course* they'd mind, so don't even ask. The same goes for their booze: your hosts won't care if you have a couple beers or make yourself a cocktail, but don't treat their liquor cabinet like it's All-You-Can-Drink Night at Señor Frog's.

If your host lives in an apartment building, use common sense. Don't be that guy on your phone in the elevator, and put garbage where garbage is supposed to go, even if it's a stinky garbage room. Hopefully, there will be a garbage chute in the hallway so you can simply drop your plastic bag into oblivion. It's kind of fun too: bye garbage!

Above all, do not—let's repeat, do not—lose your host's keys or lock yourself out in the city. Hearing the door slam behind you when keyless is one of the worst sounds known to man. Once you hear that click, you are helpless in a hallway, and nobody can hear you scream (except for that lady in 4C who is always looking out her peephole). Soon there will be a zillion voice messages, knocks on strangers' doors, talks with the building's super, and an expensive locksmith, and, worst of all, you become a *major* pain in the ass to your host. Locking yourself out is one of the biggest mistakes a city houseguest can make. It's right up there with starting a grease fire and asking your host if their thirty-thousand-dollar custom cabinets came from IKEA.

When you're a city houseguest, you walk a difficult line, as you want to stay out of your host's way while not seeming like the Unabomber locked away in your room. If possible, try to get up around the same time as your host, but if they're one of those people who goes jogging at 5:00 a.m., you're excused. Also, chitchat in the morning isn't required in the city; let the *Today Show* handle that. Your host will be fine with you simply drinking coffee together and the occasional "humf" at something in the news. If they subscribe to an actual newspaper, allow your host to read it first. A thumbed-through Metro section can suck a little joy out of a morning.

Your hosts may be genuinely interested in your plans during your stay, but they don't expect (or want) to spend every moment with you. Assume you're on your own when it comes to meals unless your host suggests meeting up. You can put out some feelers, but if you sense your host already has plans, do not beg or even strongly hint for an invitation. Make it clear that your host is welcome to join *you* on any of your plans while in the city, but when asked, if they hesitate for even a moment or use the phrase "Let's play it by ear," take that as a gargantuan NO. They've eaten a hotdog at Wrigley Field; you go knock yourself out.

Despite your host saying "If you need anything, give a shout," don't bother them at work unless it's an emergency. And, no, their Hulu password is not an emergency. If there's an appliance at their place that's difficult to operate, wait till they get home to ask about it. Go buy coffee at the deli instead of destroying their thousand-dollar espresso maker.

The length of time you're allowed to stay is also tricky. Some hosts are more laid back and genuinely don't mind if you stay a week or so if you behave like an actual adult, while others get a bit prickly after one night.

The latter type of host usually asks up front how long you will be staying, so you'll have a pretty good idea before you arrive.

Oh, and when you're ready to leave, strip the bedding off your bed, air mattress, couch, or race car and put it with the host's laundry. It's hard to understand why guests forget to do this. Even typing the words "dirty sheets" feels gross.

A SLOW BURN

—Mark S., London, England

There are two kinds of people in life: ice cube makers and ice cube takers. Ice cube makers always refill an ice cube tray with water immediately after using and place it back in the freezer, while ice cube takers take the ice they need and put the tray back in the freezer empty, never having it cross their little minds to refill the tray for the next person. I like to think I surround myself with the cube makers, those who remember there are others in the world besides themselves, who try to be considerate at least about 87.5 percent of the time. I realize I've been lucky to have these thoughtful humans in my life. However, occasionally a cube *taker* manages to hide their true stripes. They run the water, *fooling* you into thinking they're refilling the tray, when it's all a clever ruse. There will be no ice when you need it, and they won't care. This brings us to Trevor, an ice cube taker who managed to slip into my life. Oh, and he almost burned my house down.

When you're an expat living in a new country, you tend to hang out with fellow expats, not because you have anything against the locals; it's just that people from your home country are usually easier to connect with. You look up friends from college, former work colleagues, and old neighbors, that kind of thing. So when my family moved to London, I mostly hung out with people I knew from back in the States. However, after a while, I decided I should branch out and make some British friends. I already knew enough people from Dallas, Chicago, and Seattle; it was time I had "mates" from places that ended in "-shire," "-briar," and "-something-wood." I met Trevor at a gallery event, and he seemed like a good guy. He knew a lot about art and new bands, had a great beard, and tied his scarf in a cool, complicated way, all things in the plus column for a suitable British friend. Trevor also showered my wife with compliments and made my kids laugh, so his new-friend-approval-process was fast-tracked.

What Trevor did for a living was never quite clear. At various times, I heard him describe himself as a stylist, a content creator, a band manager, a photographer, a branding specialist, a producer, a gallerist, and an entrepreneur. He often took mysterious phone calls that required lots of outdoor whispering, so I never pressed him on the topic. I did know that his lifestyle exceeded his finances, and I didn't mind helping him out from time to time. This wasn't like Adam Sandler buying all his pals Maseratis, but if a friend is having a rough patch and you're in the position to help, you try to do what you can. Keep those ice trays full, I say.

My family and I were going to Australia for a few weeks, and Trevor was in a need of a place to stay, as he was "between flats." We had a small room with a bath above the garage that was separate from the house that we used primarily for visiting family. Trevor asked whether he could stay above the garage while we were away, and we agreed. He needed somewhere to stay while he looked for a new place, and he could also keep an eye on things and bring in any packages and mail while we were traveling. It was a win-win for everybody.

Before we left, we gave Trevor instructions and all contact numbers and keys he might need while we were away. My wife was a bit apprehensive, but I assured her that a forty-year-old man was more than capable of managing things in our absence. Besides, he was staying above the garage and would need to go in the house only in case of emergency, so everything would be exactly as we left it when we returned.

During the first week of our trip, we heard from Trevor only twice. Once was when a box marked "perishable" had arrived and he texted to see whether I wanted it put in the garage or taken inside the house to be refrigerated, and the other time was when he asked whether there was a garden hose. Things seemed to be going smoothly back in London, and we had nothing to worry about. (Cue ominous music.)

On day eleven of our vacation, I woke in the middle of the night to a flashing call on my phone. There had been four previous calls that I'd slept through, and all were from our security system company back in London. "Yes, hello?" I said, sitting up in bed. (I learned a call from a security company instantly makes you wide-awake.) "Sir, just wanted to let you know the house has been secured, and the fire rescue unit has been dispatched," said the security company man, thousands of miles away in London. "What's happened? What's going on? I'm not at home. I'm in Australia. There's a fire?" I said, freaking out. "Australia, that's far away. Well, I'm not at the scene, sir. I'm the dispatcher, over in Clerkenwell. I was told to reach you at this number," he said calmly. "Is the house on fire? Was there a break-in?" I said, my wife now fully awake next to me. "I'm not exactly sure, sir. As I said, I'm over in Clerkenwell, and I was told to inform you that the matter is being handled," he said, keeping calm and carrying on. "But what's happened?" I said, still totally in the dark, literally and figuratively. "I'll try to get more information; shall I ring you back at this number?" he said. "Yes, please," I said, still in freak-out mode, as we hung up. "Call Trevor!' my wife said, jumping out of bed and turning on the lights. When I called Trevor, it went straight to voicemail. I tried six more times till he groggily answered. "Yeah," he said. "Trevor, what's going on? I just got a call from the security company," I said, my wife next to me, miming things to ask. "Was there a fire? Is the house OK?" A million different scenarios ran through my mind: gas explosion, chimney fire, a family of foxes chewing through electrical wires—it is England. "Bloody hell," he replied. "I am so sorry, mate," he said, sounding like he may be drunk or crying or both.

"WHAT HAPPENED?" I yelled, now putting him on speaker in response to my wife's miming.

"The house is OK; it's OK. It's the tree," he said in almost a whisper. The tree? There were a lot of trees near the house; maybe one blew down in a storm and somehow started a fire. "Well, I was sitting outside looking up at the stars, having a late-night cigar. Before I went off to bed, I stubbed the cigar out in a knot in the tree," he continued. "What tree?" I said, still confused. "The apple tree, on the patio," he said. "I guess the cigar wasn't completely out." The tree he was referring to was a beautiful two-hundred-year-old apple tree that sat on a flagstone patio leading from the French doors of our dining room. The tree was sort of the focal point of the back of the house, providing shade in the summer and sweet-smelling blossoms in the spring and attracting countless interesting birds throughout the year. I asked Trevor to send me a photo of the tree, and he did. The tree was now a sad, gnarled, blackened stump. It reminded me of that mean tree in *The Wizard of Oz* that threw apples at Dorothy and the Scarecrow, only meaner. I also saw scorch marks on the back of the house, indicating that we were very lucky that the whole house didn't go up in flames as well.

Trevor continued to apologize, calling what happened "a freak accident," and we both agreed it was probably best he find somewhere else to stay. I arranged for a neighbor friend to check out the damage, collect the keys from Trevor, and report back. After my neighbor went to our house, he sent us photos of the interior, which now looked like the aftermath of a frat party and a tornado, which my wife dubbed the "fratnado." Trevor did not stay over the garage, as we discussed, but had taken over the house. There were dirty dishes, empty liquor bottles, cigarette butts, and overflowing garbage in the trash bins. The beds had all been slept in as well, so we assumed that he had guests (he denied this) or that Goldilocks had paid a visit and tried out each room. When confronted about the state of the house, Trevor downplayed things and said he had just come in to use the kitchen a couple times. He offered to pay for any damages and cleaning, but since he had no money, we both knew that wasn't going to happen.

The rest of my time in Australia was preoccupied with worrying about the house and feeling like an idiot for having trusted someone who let me down big-time. Once back home, I discovered that all the booze Trevor (and whoever?) drank came from my house. Gift bottles of champagne, wine brought back from trips, the top-shelf liquor we were going to get to someday—all gone. I also learned that the cigar Trevor used to ignite the apple tree came from a humidor on my desk, a humidor that was now just an empty box that mocked me. I smoked one cigar maybe every six months; he wiped them all out in a little over a week. How was that possible? Did he have a baby and give them out to people? I'll never know.

I had tree people come out to look at what remained of the apple tree to see whether it could be saved, but it was a lost cause and they had to remove it. I also had patio people come to assess the damage to the flagstone and was told that most of it had cracked as a result of heat damage and would have to be replaced. They also kept commenting on how it was a miracle the house wasn't in ashes as well.

In addition to having the tree and patio stone removed, I also removed Trevor from my life. The last we chatted was when I told him I would no longer be keeping him on my Friends and Family phone plan. He was actually a bit surprised. "I didn't realize it was that much of an imposition" were his exact words, I believe.

On the day the tree and patio people came to the house, I really needed a drink after they left. I found a bottle of scotch in the back of the cabinet with all the breakfast cereal that apparently Trevor and company missed. I was angry and embarrassed and didn't want to think about it all anymore. I grabbed a glass and opened open the freezer to get some ice but . . .

You know, sometimes, it's good to drink it neat.

CHAPTER 2

GETTING SOME AIR

The Country Houseguest

Y ou love staring at that tree outside your window. You get all excited when its buds arrive in spring and get a little bummed in autumn when it turns into a tall, sad, gray thing. This tree is your friend that helps you keep track of the seasons; it says good morning to you each day and doesn't judge you late at night when you stumble home after accidentally having too much rosé. You were even going to download an app to find out what kind of tree it is, but then you watched another episode of *The Bear* and forgot about it. Sure, bringing your own bags to the supermarket proves you're doing everything possible to save the environment, but your bond with this tree demonstrates that your connection with nature goes deeper. Well, get ready to have your mind blown, because there's a place where there are tons of these green sprouting wonders: it's called the *country*, and you've been invited to visit.

The country is always a great escape from the city. Each time you visit, you pause in front of a real estate office window to stare at photos of fixer-uppers and imagine leaving your current life behind and moving to the country. You tell yourself, "I'll buy a little house here and open a bookstore or maybe a shop that sells only brooms." Then you remember there isn't a Starbucks for thirty miles and walk away.

As a guest in the country, you get to wear all those clothes you feel ridiculous wearing in the city. Drag out that quilted plaid vest and those rubber Wellie boots you bought because Kate Middleton wore them and feel free to wear anything flannel, tweed, or puffy. You're in the land of burrs and prickly bush things, so your time here can be a full-on Patagonia-palooza. However, if possible, avoid wearing anything fleece— it's so Ted Cruz on the weekend.

When you first see your guest room, you'll probably get a little choked up. Patchwork quilts, rugs woven from rags, a lamp made out of a bird house. The adorable level will be through the roof, and you'll make a mental note to finally finish watching that Hallmark movie where a plucky gal returns to her hometown to run her family's fudge company. However, once you've settled in to your room, you might realize that not everything is exactly perfect. Remember: this is the country and the house is old, so if the electrical outlet next to the bed doesn't work, suck it up. And, wait, where's the air conditioner? Open a window! If it won't stay open, just prop it up with a weathered copy of a James Patterson novel. By law, every guest room has to have at least one. Sure, the dresser drawers stick, the light in the bathroom is out, and there are only three hangers in the closet. There is no concierge to call, so be a good guest and try to fix whatever's wrong yourself. Your hosts don't need to be reminded that "the wind sure whistles through that cracked pane of glass in the window over the bed." This is their house, and they are well aware of the whistle, so find some duct tape and move on.

Things with four legs or more are another factor you'll encounter as a country guest. Yes, you'll squeal, "Look, a bunny!" and scream, "Stop the car, oh my God, it's a family of pheasants!" but you might also squeal when you spot some other things as well. These are little surprises like spiders, mice, centipedes, frogs, and a myriad of other creepy-crawly things at every turn. This is the country, these things live here, and you're invading *their* turf, so learn to peacefully coexist. A daddy longlegs in the shower isn't going to kill you, and the chipmunk staring you down on the front porch only wants your granola bar. So be a good guest and keep your insect/arachnid/rodent hysteria to a minimum. Also, so as not to bother your hosts, bring your own bug spray for black flies and mosquitos. They are really awful, and you're totally allowed to hate them.

This seems like a good time to talk about a topic that you won't be able to avoid as a guest in the country. A topic that elicits more anxiety than turbulence on an Aeroflot flight and puts your host and everyone else on high alert. It's discussed at the gas station, fancy dinner parties, and the roadside stand with the good cherries. The topic is TICKS. These little suckers (literally) are parasites that live off your blood and can leave behind a charming condition called Lyme disease. Not to get all Sanjay Gupta on you, but you do not want Lyme disease. It's terrible and debilitating and can screw you up for a long time. So if your host seems a bit overzealous in their warnings—telling you to wear long pants, to coat yourself in DEET, and to always check yourself for any ticks after a day outdoors—listen to them. Think of the country as *The Walking Dead*, and the ticks are the Walkers: they are to be feared.

Technology in the country can prove a little challenging. Your host may mention that the power goes out occasionally, so don't freak out if it does. Candles and flashlights are kind of fun, and it usually comes back on in an hour or two. However, if it stays out longer than that, you are allowed to start worrying about meat in the refrigerator, but not out loud. Nobody wants to be labeled a meat worrier.

Cell service and Wi-Fi connections can also be a bit problematic in the country. Your host may suggest leaning out a window or standing on a chair in your room to get reception. If it works, do it! Better than driving thirty miles to that Starbucks.

Your host might have relationships with locals that you may find surprising. For instance, if they introduce you to a tattoo-covered gentleman named Dusty with a limited number of teeth, nod politely. Dusty fixes their roof and clears wasps' nests from their gutters, and while he may not seem like someone your host would normally be friends with, they genuinely like him, so don't be a dismissive visiting city person. When Vicky, their vaguely racist neighbor, stops by with some jam she made, don't blanch at every F-bomb she drops. This is the country, and things operate a little differently here. You let people into your life who may not be the same as those in your usual social circle, and that's a good thing. Not everyone in the world has to own something from Banana Republic.

You'll have a great time in the country if you relax and go with the flow. Try to show enthusiasm for things you normally wouldn't back home. When your host gives you a tour of their garden and goes on about how *fertile* their soil is, ask questions—and, yes, you must marvel at the size of their zucchini and heirloom tomatoes. "Go on, you've had NO formal gardening training?" You'll also learn more about composting than you ever thought possible, so seem genuinely interested in the fact that coffee grounds and eggshells are great for the compost while sawdust is not, and if they ramble on wayyyyyy too long, fall back on that always-useful phrase, "Look, a bunny!"

FARROW & BALL GUEST ROOM PAINT COLOR or STING SONG?

1. January Stars
2. When Dolphins Dance
3. After The Rain Has Fallen
4. Mouse's Back
5. August Winds
6. All Four Seasons
7. Vert De Terre
8. Another Pyramid
9. Arsenic
10. Christmas at Sea
11. Savage Ground
12. Clear or cloudy
13. London Stone
14. Charlotte's Locks
15. Tea In The Sahara
16. Pointing
17. Dead Man's Boots
18. Desert Rose
19. Lichen
20. Ghost Story
21. Elephant's breath
22. Troublemaker
23. Green Smoke
24. Moon Over Bourbon Street
25. Saint Augustine In Hell
26. Matchstick

ANSWERS:

FARROW & BALL COLOR 4, 7, 9, 11, 13, 14, 16, 19, 21, 23, 26   STING SONG 1, 2, 3, 5, 6, 8, 10, 12, 15, 17, 18, 20, 22, 24, 25

CHAPTER 3

GOING GLOBAL
The Houseguest Abroad

When you're planning your next trip and realize you've already been to most of the good states (do you really need to see *both* Dakotas?), it's time to grab your passport and head somewhere that embraces the metric system and asymmetrical haircuts.

If you're invited to be a houseguest in another country, accept, but don't seem overly eager. The host extending the invitation most likely invited you thinking you'd never actually fly thousands of miles to visit. The distance between you and someone's guest room allows them to seem gracious without ever having to fluff the futon. So be nonchalant and say things like, "Dubrovnik in the spring sounds wonderful, but when will I find the time?" Then immediately go to the bathroom and start searching for cheap flights to Croatia. If you seem too eager and immediately press your host for specific dates, it gives them the opportunity to backpedal on their invitation. They might suddenly remember they're having their septic system completely rebuilt. An element of surprise works in your favor. Call your hosts (harder to weasel out of than an email) and say you'll be traveling and that if your schedule "works out," you were thinking of dropping by to visit.

Never give an exact number of days you'll be staying and always make it seem like you have somewhere to go before and after visiting them, even though you have zero other plans. International travel guarantees added time to your stay, and the farther the distance you travel, the harder it is for your host to kick you out. Who goes to New Zealand for just a couple days besides flight attendants and Bono?

Whether your host is an expat or native to where you're visiting will affect your houseguest experience. Expat hosts love to demonstrate they've totally embraced their new culture and have somehow forgotten practically everything about America. It's as if they received a Jedi mind wipe once they passed through immigration. They'll feign ignorance of American customs, vocabulary, and cultural references and will make statements such as "Looks like rain; we'll probably need a *guarda-chuva*" and "This Gilligan you speak of, you say he had an *island*?" Play along, and do not point out that it's odd they have a heavy accent after living abroad for three months (see: Lohan, Lindsay, post move to Dubai). Instead, make it appear that you, too, are eager to leave your Yankee ways behind. Ask their advice and pretend to be impressed at how quickly they've assimilated. Then say you need to get some air and go directly to McDonald's.

Native hosts try very hard to make you feel at home. They'll go out of their way to surprise you with things they assume all Americans love. They are making an effort, so you should as well. Act genuinely thrilled when they serve you a cocktail made from Malibu rum and Diet Mountain Dew and marvel at the hot pink Crocs they left in your guest room. Native hosts view American houseguests as novelties, like squirrels who can water ski, and they like to show them off. If a dinner party is planned in your honor, remember that people outside the USA actually *know* things—things like how to pronounce Qatar, Namibia, and Saoirse Ronan. So maybe brush up on general knowledge before your trip. You don't want to be the only person at the dinner table whose political insight is limited to the fact that France has a hot president.

If your host asks you to join them in their plans, you must go and go enthusiastically, no matter how odd their plans may sound. Chances are they won't include you in everything, so suck it up and go—don't be that American jerk who came to visit. Christmas fairs, catacomb tours, sad war memorials, experimental jazz clubs . . . you're going. All right, if they suggest experimental jazz, you don't have to go; nobody should have to listen to someone play a toy piano with a hammer.

When you're a houseguest abroad, in a way, you're an ambassador for the USA. This is your chance to represent America in a positive light. It's like you're an Olympic athlete but without the 5:00 a.m. training sessions and eventually competing on *Dancing with the Stars*. Other countries look different, sound different, and smell different; that's why we travel. Who would want a world that's one giant Cinnabon? OK, probably a lot of people. When you're a houseguest abroad, it might take a little getting used to things. You're allowed to giggle at the bathroom bidet, but only once, and *never* use the phrase "At home, we call that a . . ." Your hosts have watched *Friends*, so they know how America works.

Whenever possible, try to dispel common misconceptions about Americans. Even if they're mostly true, there's no need to beat a dead horse. First, stop screaming. Americans are loud. If you notice your host jumps a little from your resounding "Good morning!" pull it back a bit. Try to use your "indoor voice," but the indoors of a library run by a librarian with severe control issues.

THE STRUGGLE IS REAL...

FIGURING OUT YOUR HOST'S SHOWER

The Silkwood

Scalding and freezing are your two water temperature options. So, if you're looking to be poached or want to induce heart failure, you're in luck.

Ex Machina

Who doesn't love listening to incessant beeping as you stand naked pushing buttons while absolutely nothing happens.

The Whac-A-mole
Turn it into a game and try to guess what will happen each time you push one of the four unmarked knobs.

Simple, but Deadly
Do I push it in or pull it out? Wait, it doesn't pull out. Hot must be to the left, no that's cold. OK, why is the tub filling up?

The Cobra
Once you untangle and wrestle with it for ten minutes, then the fun starts as it sprays all over the bathroom.

Americans also have the reputation for being know-it-alls. If your host is giving you a tour of their city or offering a little background on their country's history, there is absolutely no reason to correct them if they get things a little confused. Does it really matter exactly when a basilica was built or how high that mountain peak really is? Nobody is ever going to say "Boy, that American sure knows his Protestant Reformation facts," so keep it to yourself.

I NEVER TOUCHED THE STRUDEL

—Andy G., Los Angeles

I stayed with my friend Johann for a week at his apartment in Berlin. These are some of the notes he left for me during my visit.

(Post-it note stuck to lamp in guest room)
"Welcome friend! The Wi-Fi password is DeFLeoPard22
The signal should be very strong. It is not right now connected to the pornography as my building management blocks. I hope that is ok."

(Note taped to the door of the refrigerator)
"Good morning! Eat any of the foods that you like. All I ask is that you do not touch the strudel. It is not mine."

(Post-it note on bathroom mirror)
"Rise and shine! The toilet has a temper, so do not flush anything that is not paper.
If you should have a 'big one,' [*wink emoji drawn*] there is a plunger in closet for use."

(Post-it note on bedroom door)
"Quick question. Do you enjoy humour?"

(Note taped to the door of the refrigerator)
"So friend, MY bad! The strudel is not actually strudel. It is called stollen, but I thought you might recognize it as strudel. Sorry for any confusion. Still, please do not touch it."

(Post-it note on my laptop)
"Something to consider, I know you may be doing Zoom calls in the mornings. Please let me know in advance, as I've been known to walk in apartment naked in the a.m. Don't want any Zoom surprises!"

(Piece of cardboard slid under guest room door)
"Morning Rockstar! There is a party tonight in honour of my friend Uli's birthday, please come along with me. The party should be great fun, Uli is bisexual. Business casual."

(Post-it note on bed headboard)
"If you are cold at night, look for extra blankets in the hall closet. One was once my former dog's, so I'd consider smelling first."

(Written on the whiteboard on the front door of the apartment)
"I have a visitor in my room, so if you hear the bed being used, that is why. I apologize for any sleep interruption. Please clean this message from board."

(Post-it note inside the refrigerator)
"Yo bro, the coast is clear and all good! Go ahead and eat the strudel."

CHAPTER 4

THE SMELL OF SUNSCREEN IN THE MORNING

The Houseguest at the Beach

Your sweat-soaked shirt clings to your back, thousand-degree car seats (black interiors = pain) pan-sear your thighs, and the city takes on that charming aroma of rotting dumpster. Ah, summer. Then, you get the call. "Why don't you come to the beach?" they say, and you know you've been rescued. No more sitting in theaters watching Vin Diesel blockbusters or repeated stopping in 7-Eleven just for the good air-conditioning—you're going to the beach!

Beach invitations are highly coveted. Your hosts could have asked anyone, but they chose you as their houseguest. And since they did, let others know it. "No, I can't make it; I'm going to the beach with friends," "Sorry, I have to leave early; I'm headed to a friend's place at the beach," and "Oh darn, that won't work; friends are expecting me . . . at the beach" are a few ways to signal to others that you'll soon be pretending you like playing Kadima somewhere near the water.

When you're a beach houseguest, good weather is never guaranteed. If you think you may go mad sitting inside watching the rain fall on a sad, gray, Bergman movie beach, check the weather forecast before you head to the shore. Your host wants houseguests who can enthusiastically play Yahtzee for six hours on a rainy day, not those who heavily sigh and check Carrot Weather every two minutes. Liquor can sometimes help you get through bad beach weather, but make sure your host is also up for alcohol-fueled fun. You don't want to be the only person playing "Every time we hear the thunder, we drink!"

Once at the beach, all you have to do is sit back and relax . . . and do everything within your power to get asked back. Having an open invitation at a beach house is your goal. Never again will you have to worry about what to do on the weekend and you can page through the J.Crew catalog swimsuit section without feeling like a fraud. However, securing your place as a reoccurring houseguest will require a bit of effort.

Finding out whether your host owns or rents where you're staying will guide you. If the house is owned, let the compliments flow. Who cares if it's a little far from town, has plumbing from the Harding administration, and a slight ant problem—it's FREE. No complaining or passive-aggressive observations, like "After a while, you barely notice the sound of that train." Even if your host makes disparaging comments about the place, do not join in. They're allowed to grumble about the "Tell-Tale Heart" dripping faucet; you are not.

However, if the place is a rental, you have a bit of leeway. Your host might want you to join in the fun as they tear into the home's stone and steel decor that suggests a Flintstones-as-coke-dealers aesthetic. Show how supportive a guest you are as you listen to their detailed thoughts on what *they* would do with the place. People love to tell others about hypothetical renovations and greatly appreciate houseguests who encourage their Sub-Zero dreams. "Yes, I'd love to hear more about a closet-turned-mudroom!"

When you're at the actual beach, there are some things to keep in mind that can also help secure your space as a reoccurring houseguest. For instance, wear sunscreen. It's not just those with skin like fine bone china that need help from the SPF gods, so slather it on. A blistered back is not an interesting topic of conversation, and watching someone peel layers of skin from their nose near the potato salad can really bring down a barbecue. Yes, we know: you have Mediterranean blood and never burn. And after your host has to drive you to the ER in the middle of the night, remember to tell that to the nurse packing you in ice.

Towels. Aside from politics, religion, and who really should have won *RuPaul's Drag Race*, few topics get people more worked up. Hosts are very particular about their towels. They have specific towels meant for the beach, while others are only for indoors, like a declawed cat. Generally, any towel that's white, monogrammed, or from the museum of towels (known as Restoration Hardware) should never touch sand. While towels that feature a giant Coca-Cola bottle, SpongeBob, or any team mascot are beach friendly.

While some hosts want the dreaded damp beach towel hung in the bathroom, many prefer that you leave it on the floor, and others may even have a designated soiled beach towel zone, as if they're contaminated and need the full *Silkwood* treatment. Hosts sometimes visibly blanch when asked what to do with a damp, sandy beach towel. They'll stammer, point in different directions, and mumble something about how you can leave it and they'll take care of it later, clearly indicating they want the whole situation to just go away. One way to minimize this pain for your host is to bring your own towels. Your host may not say anything, but they will absolutely notice and make a mental note that the houseguest who brought their own terry cloth is on the "gets to come back" list.

If looking for a topic that's sure to make everyone uncomfortable, it's what to wear at the beach. As a houseguest, this is not your time to be a fashion maverick. You want to blend in among the other beach-goers and wear nothing that draws attention. This is not Ibiza. You're sitting among people reading the latest Jodi Picoult and hordes of children tormenting hermit crabs, so leave that swimsuit that came in a tube at home. You do not want to end up on somebody's Instagram under the hashtag #beachfreak, #thongsowrong, or #unsafeatanySpeedo. Wear what would be acceptable poolside at a Marriott—and not one of those new fancy Marriotts either.

You should not wear anything that would force your host to have to explain your appearance to friends who do an umbrella drop-by while you're hanging out at the beach. Reconsider your beachwear if it can be described as, or features, any of the following: mesh, translucent, edible, clingy, Swarovski crystals, fishnet, Amish inspired, hard R, feathers, peek-a-boo, magnets, pleather, *Love Island*-esque, tassels, dungeon friendly, bum-tastic, or French.

CHAPTER 5

YOU CAN GO HOME AGAIN . . . IT'S JUST REALLY, REALLY WEIRD

Staying with Family

"You can do this—seriously, you can. No, you can't; you'll go crazy in ten minutes. But it's only for a few days, so how bad could it be? Bad, like really bad, like ending up sedated and strapped to a gurney bad." This has been a brief internal monologue many have had before staying with family. There's really no good way to prepare for being a houseguest with relatives. Sure, knowing there's some Xanax in your travel bag helps, but when you stay with family, there are always a few surprises.

The first thing you'll learn upon arriving is whatever the current family drama is and whom it involves. Usually, someone is not talking to someone else, because of something someone supposedly said, when they probably didn't say it in the first place. That doesn't matter; this is *family*, so all rules of reason are out the window. You might ask a relative an innocuous question, like "So how's Wendy doing?" only to be met with an icy stare and a reply of "Oh, so now *you're* siding with Wendy!" When in fact you are not siding with Wendy; you have no idea what is going on, and you were only making conversation, because, frankly, you could not give a monkey's ass about how Wendy is doing. In order to be a good family houseguest, your goal is to avoid all conflict. When a family member unloads every last detail of their latest suburban drama—despite claiming they don't want to talk about it—say nothing. Absolutely nothing. Offer no opinions; do not sympathize; ask no questions; do not nod, shrug your shoulders, or widen your eyes, all of which could be construed as either agreeing or disagreeing with what's been said. If you momentarily delude yourself into thinking maybe you could help solve the situation, remind yourself that this is *family* you're dealing with here. You can't win. You can love these people and wish the best for them, but you can't help, and they don't want you to. You are merely a guest in their world, and once you sense the speaker has stopped talking, calmly head toward your guest room and shut your door. An open door could easily invite a few more details about Wendy.

If visiting your parents, you'll most likely be staying in the room that was once your childhood bedroom. Sure, that Portishead poster is still on the wall, but you'll soon discover things have changed. When you open your old sock drawer, you'll find it's now filled with ten bags of walnuts. "They were on sale at Costco." And when you look in the closet, don't be surprised to find a collection of things straight out of the *Silence of the Lambs* storage unit. "Your father and his garage sales!"

The temperature of your room will be one of two extremes: either so ungodly hot that you could grow orchids or so cold that your shampoo is semi-frozen into a Slurpee-like state. You'll be offered countless blankets, comforters, and additional pillows. Take them all, as you can use them to block heat vents or air-conditioning units and hopefully create an environment livable for humans.

There's also a chance that your bedroom has now been repurposed and transformed into something else. It might now be some odd hybrid— half scrapbooking room/half home gym—or maybe the walls are now lined with aquariums. Though to your parents it's still your bedroom, so you'll be sleeping there. Your parents are proud of what they've done with the room, so make sure to compliment their efforts as you stumble over dumbbells and gag on the smell of guppy food.

Assume all electronics in your room will not function properly, as they either are ancient or have been jerry-rigged with tape, tin foil, and the occasional chip clip, so that attempting to use them will put your life at risk. If asked why you're not watching television, say you're happy reading, versus the fact that sparks flew out of back of the set when you turned it on. Again, avoid all conflict. If you told the truth about the television, you'd be labeled a "snob" and be informed, "Well, it works perfectly fine for everybody else."

One of the most mystifying things you'll encounter when a houseguest with family is the pursuit of their Wi-Fi password. Oh, they definitely have one, but they guard it like it's the nuclear codes and the truth of whether Ronan Farrow is truly Frank Sinatra's son. (He really looks like him, doesn't he?) Since they guard it, they also lose it, so factor in a good forty-five minutes of searching time. "Wait, no, that's either my bicycle lock combination or your mother's blood pressure." When they finally locate the password, written on a torn piece of a Captain Crunch box taped inside a kitchen cabinet, it will be the original password supplied by the internet provider and contain at least thirty case-sensitive characters, some possibly cuneiform.

Meals must be eaten with your family. Even if you have plans to eat later, you must sit at the table and pretend to enjoy whatever is placed before you. If you're vegan or have any other dietary restrictions, it won't matter. They might even acknowledge you don't eat meat as they slop beef stroganoff on your plate, because in their minds those rules don't apply when you're with family. It's much easier to just pretend you're eating rather than having it become a thing. Watch a couple Nancy Meyers movies for help with fake eating techniques. In her cashmere shawl/ expensive kitchen movies, people are often moving food around their plates, cutting it up, and even placing mostly empty forks in their mouth; you do the same.

Another topic that could easily lead to conflict when staying with family is politics. Of course, politics can be a volatile topic with most people; however, with family it's different. You grew up with these people and assumed they shared your same core beliefs, so when you realize they've somehow wandered into the valley of conspiracy theories, it can be unnerving. But again, say nothing, as a rational political discussion with family is not remotely within the realm of possibility. It would suddenly turn from a debate of differing political ideologies to why YOU got a ten-speed bike for Christmas when they really wanted one.

When you're a houseguest with family, you want to slip in and out with zero controversy. It can be a genuinely positive experience—honest. Simply steer clear of any topics that are likely to stir things up, especially from the past, and if your buttons are pushed, take it in stride . . . or take a Xanax. Remember that somewhere else you have a full, interesting life to return to, while their life is here . . . with Wendy.

THE SPY WHO DIDN'T LOVE ME

—Sarah J., Camden, Maine

My brother Brian never really dated much, as he was always obsessed with his career. So my husband, Mark, and I were thrilled when he told us he was coming to visit us in Maine with his new girlfriend. We didn't know much about her except that her name was Natalia and she worked in fashion in New York City. I immediately started to worry that this glamorous big-city lady might take exception with my around-the-house uniform of sweatpants and a Smashing Pumpkins T-shirt. I decided to up my game by putting a new scrunchie in my hair.

Brian and Natalia arrived late on Friday night. Natalia seemed quiet at first, but when I look back on it now, I think she was silently assessing the room, looking for the weakest member of the herd. She was pretty, with a grown-up version of Dora the Explorer's haircut. Natalia wore a lot—I mean a lot—of makeup (I'm not saying this to be catty; it plays a role in the story) and spoke with a pronounced Russian accent, because, it turns out, she was from Russia. Though it would have been a better story if she wasn't.

I asked how their drive up was, and she shrugged, then looked at my brother and said "Snawpple." That was the first word she said, and she would say it often during their stay. When Brian first told me they were coming, I asked if there was anything Natalia might want me to pick up at the grocery store. I thought she could be gluten free or vegan or something. He emailed me a rather specific list that included white chocolate hazelnut Coffee-Mate creamer, pineapple (rings, not whole), Jimmy Dean breakfast sausage, and Diet Peach Snapple (Snawpple), which was her beverage of choice. Whenever Natalia wanted one, she would bark

"Snawpple," and whoever was in the room, usually my brother or me, was expected to bring her one.

Due to Natalia's whole "Boris and Natasha" vibe and, um, abrupt manner, Mark and I dubbed her The Spy. She would interrogate you more than have a conversation. "Why live Maine? Cold and far from good stores." If someone told me she had a dagger strapped to her leg under her Juicy Couture tracksuit, I would have absolutely believed them.

The Saturday morning after they arrived, Mark and Brian went to play golf, and Natalia slept late. I was busy getting things ready for a party I was throwing for Mark's birthday on Sunday. It was a milestone birthday, so it was going to be a pretty big event with a band, bartenders, and probably around fifty people. When Natalia came downstairs to the kitchen at around eleven, I had coffee and her hazelnut creamer all ready for her. When I asked how she slept, she replied, "Awful. Mattress terrible." I ignored her and kept on arranging flowers in a vase for the party. She was slumped in a chair drinking her coffee, and I thought I'd try to make small talk. "So what's your favorite flower?" I asked. She gave a throaty little laugh and replied, "Not those," then stood up and shuffled from the room back upstairs. OK, you can slam my state and insult my mattress, but nobody makes fun of my flowers. Gardening is my one hobby that takes me to my happy place, and I grew all those flowers from tiny baby seedlings, so, yes, maybe I'm a little overly sensitive about them. I wasn't going to confront Natalia about her comment, but I knew one thing: from now on, somebody was going to be getting their own Snawpple.

The rest of the day went fine. The guys came back from golf, and we had a little backyard barbecue. My brother and Natalia seemed to be fighting a lot, but I assumed she probably had told him to move the sun thirty degrees or have the birds stop chirping so loudly and was not happy when he couldn't. The only things that seemed to make Natalia happy were shopping and Harry Styles, whom she called "my boyfriend." Great, now

I'd never be able to listen to "Watermelon Sugar" again. I could not figure out what my brother saw in her, until later that afternoon when they took a nap and I heard noises coming from their guest room that a sister should never hear. It sounded like somebody was in a bear trap.

I got up early on Sunday, as it was time to go into full party planning mode. I would be going nonstop until guests arrived. I started by doing laundry and getting the bathrooms in order. As I took my white guest towels from the bathroom hamper, I discovered they were no longer white, as Natalia had smeared several layers of her makeup all over them. My once pristine towels were now covered in foundation, bronzer, lipstick, eye shadow, mascara, and who knows what else. I held one up, and it looked like the Shroud of Turin.

As I headed downstairs to the laundry room with the towels, I ran into Natalia, who was on her way up with coffee. I was quite proud that I managed to maintain my composure, smile, and not push her down the stairs, but I knew I had to say something. So in as pleasant a voice as I could muster, I said, "Hey, Natalia, I have some wipes and cotton balls and stuff to take off your makeup, so then you won't have to use the towels. I'll put it all in the bathroom." I thought what I said sounded genuine, helpful, and only mildly passive-aggressive. She brushed past me without acknowledging me.

As I walked into the kitchen, I found Mark standing at the island looking down at a huge mess on the counter. Things were cut up; there were knives, a strainer, and various glasses. "What the hell is this?" he said. At first I was confused, and then I realized what it was and almost cried. As I mentioned, gardening is my thing, and it was my mother's as well. A few years before she died, we went on a trip to France together and both took home oranges we found on the grounds of the Palace of Versailles. We were convinced customs agents were going to arrest us for bringing stolen oranges into the country, and our "fruit-smuggling" caper became a running joke between us. After our trip, we both planted seeds from our oranges, and they grew into little trees that we kept in pots in our kitchens. After Mom was gone, I took her tree to my house. My tree grew some blossoms, but that was about it; however, after years of patience and care, Mom's tree eventually would produce two or three weird little oranges a year. It was like she came to visit when they arrived. There had been two oranges this year, both of which had been growing nicely . . . until they were yanked from the little tree and now sat mangled and massacred on the kitchen counter. Natalia had decided to try to make orange juice.

OK, then I did cry. I knew it was silly to cry over a couple oranges, but c'mon! Mark calmed me down, and I decided I would not turn this into a big thing and ruin the party. I would have a little "chat" with my brother later about the orange slaughterer. Right now, my mantra became "Focus on chilling the rosé . . . focus on chilling the rosé."

The party had a tropical theme. I know it's a little overplayed, but when you live in Maine, you do anything you can to get people out of fleece. The party was going pretty well. I was busy greeting guests, passing hors d'oeuvres, and occasionally dancing to the calypso band who did a surprisingly impressive rendition of "Suffragette City." I had totally forgotten about Natalia till I looked across the yard and saw her coming out of the house. She had embraced the tropical theme with a flowing off-the-shoulder sundress and by ripping the head off one of my beloved Casablanca lilies from the garden and putting it behind her ear.

A little later as I moved through the crowd, I saw Brian and Natalia arguing. Apparently, he had been talking to a pretty female guest, and Natalia was not happy about it. Soon things went very Jerry Springer and a drink was thrown. I didn't want the situation to get any uglier and decided I would diffuse the drama with a tray of scallops wrapped in bacon. Bacon-wrapped scallops should snap anyone back to behaving like a normal person, right? As I walked to Brian and Natalia and presented the tray, I went a full octave higher than my normal voice. "Hey, guys, bacon-wrapped scallops! Get 'em while they're hot!" At that moment Natalia, who was then screeching at my brother, turned around and slapped me across the face. I'm guessing it was about a 7.2 on the Will Smith face-slapping scale. Down to the ground fell the scallops as I held my face in disbelief. If I recall correctly, the band was playing "The Tide Is High."

Brian and Natalia did not stay the night. They would break up about two months later. Soon after, someone would slash Brian's tires.

Last anyone heard, Natalia was dating a New York Ranger.

HOME ALONE
The House-Sitting Houseguest

If you're invited to stay at someone else's home when they're not in town, you've scored big-time. There's no walking on eggshells when you have the whole place to yourself, and with any luck, they have one of those crazy comfortable Swedish mattresses and get all the premium channels you don't. Will you find time to watch all five seasons of *The Handmaid's Tale* during your stay? Absolutely.

There are two different types of house-sitting experiences, both of which can be outstanding. In one, you are asked by the host to take care of their place while they're away and are expected to perform a few duties while they're gone. This situation is especially good if their place is in the same city where you live and it's much nicer than your own. Hello, washer and dryer IN the apartment; nice to meet you, refrigerator with working ice maker; the pleasure is all mine, rain showerhead with insanely strong water pressure.

When you agree to house-sit for your host and perform some tasks, you should view these duties like a job, so imitate a responsible adult and don't blow them off. Water the plants per instructions, take in the mail daily, and if any packages arrive, put them where your host will easily find them. If there are animals to care for, feed them on schedule and hang out with them. The poor dog or cat is no doubt freaked out wondering who this unknown human is in their house, so make an effort to become friends. They might seem disinterested or skittish at first, but you'll feel like the Pet Whisperer when Baxter or Pepper finally decides you're not totally horrible and jumps on your bed.

If your host asks you to walk the dog three times a day, do that and go for legitimate walks; don't just let them do their bidniz then bring them back inside. Also, bring poop bags along on walks, unless you want to be chased down the street by the neighborhood poop monitor and have them report back to your host that their dog was breaking the law. If there are more exotic pets (lizards, tropical fish, birds, etc.), make sure you are up to dealing with them as they may require more specialized care. If feeding a defrosted frozen mouse on a stick to a snake would (understandably) freak you out, maybe pass on house-sitting this time.

In the other house-sitting situation, the host doesn't ask you to perform any duties but gives you the keys to their place and trusts you with it when they're not there. This could be their primary residence or a vacation home; either way, they're being ridiculously generous, so make sure not to take advantage of things. Leave everything in the condition you found it or in some cases even better. Straighten up whatever rooms need it, and if the bathroom could use a good cleaning, break out the Scrubbing Bubbles, or if the throw rugs look extra dusty, take them outside for a thorough beating. No need to worry that your housekeeping efforts will offend your host by suggesting they're slobs; nobody on the planet would ever object to somebody else cleaning their toilet. If your host lets you use their car, fill it up with gas before leaving and be extra careful when driving. Washing the car would also earn you major good houseguest points.

In both house-sitting scenarios, there some other things to consider. Getting the keys to your host's place should be rather easy, but it can be tricky, especially if your host will not be at home when you arrive or if they don't have an extra set. Never make things difficult for your host in terms of the key exchange. Always agree with whatever way they suggest, even if it inconveniences you a little. They're nice enough to let you stay in their home, so you can take a cab to their office to pick up the keys. If they have a doorman or a neighbor who will hand off the keys, you're in luck. However, if you have to rely on a fake rock with a key inside or a key left under a flower pot, triple-check as to where that rock is located and exactly which flower pot they mean before you arrive. Ask your host to send you a photo of where they put the key, as this will avoid any key confusion later. Attempting to climb through a window as a patrol car pulls up isn't a great way to start your stay.

When it comes to food, you're allowed to eat and drink anything in the refrigerator, within reason, and your hosts will probably encourage you to do so. However, popping open that bottle of Veuve Clicquot or deciding to grill the filet mignon in the freezer is taking things a little far. If you run out of staples like coffee, butter, or breakfast cereal, replace them before you leave. One morning, when all your host wants more than anything in the world is a bowl of Cinnamon Toast Crunch, they'd be bummed to find the empty box.

Depending on how long you're staying, you should be conscious of the heat and air-conditioning. Unless it gets super hot or cold, keep it at the temperature your host has set it to. If you need to adjust it, make sure to put it back to where it was before you leave. A lot of the time it's easier to open a window or put on a sweater instead of having to deal with a complicated thermostat that won't stop beeping and that you're worried you probably broke.

If you have a friend in the area, you can invite them over, but don't turn it into a party; your Ferris Bueller days are over. It's *not* cool to invite random people you just meet online to your host's place, as it's rude and creepy. If anything from the place was damaged or went missing, you'd be mortified, and despite that really deep ten-minute texting conversation you had with them, they're strangers. Don't you watch *Dateline*?

When you're alone at someone's house, you'll inevitably get curious about their lives. You'll notice the books on their shelves, see what shows are in their Netflix history, and learn they like gin instead of vodka from the bottles on their bar. All this is perfectly fine and not an invasion of their privacy; other things, well, that's different. If bringing in the mail, do that and nothing else. Don't look through it and absolutely do not open anything. Put all the mail in a bag or box and be done with it. Don't bother perusing their catalogs either; you already know everything that's sold at Williams-Sonoma and L.L.Bean.

Wearing your host's clothing is also not allowed. Sure, if it's raining, you can throw on a slicker, but no going through drawers or closets. It's wrong on a lot of levels. They'll know you wore it, too—they just will.

You will try not to look in your host's medicine cabinet, but since we are all flawed humans, you will eventually succumb to curiosity and take a peek. Though you are not allowed to take anything from the cabinet, aside from maybe a Band-Aid. This especially applies to pharmaceuticals. Most normal people are aware of this, but there are those who think "borrowing" a pill or three is no big deal. It is, and if you do it, you're no longer a houseguest but now a criminal with a key to your host's front door.

CHAPTER 7

ISLAND LIFE
The Tropical Houseguest

It might take eleven hours, three planes, a canoe, a bus, and a donkey to get there, but if someone invites you to their place on a tropical island, you're going. Oh yes, you are definitely going. This isn't like getting invited to your cousin's condo in Sarasota. You've scored an invitation to someplace you aren't even sure how to pronounce, let alone locate where it is on a map. It doesn't matter what it takes; you're going to find a way to get there.

Once you arrive, your host will point out this isn't some place that everyone has been to and act as if they're the one who discovered it. They view themselves as Columbus in Ray-Bans, so let them. Your host is the ultimate expert on this paradise you're visiting, so say things like "Wow," "Amazing," and "No way" when they tell you about the Michelin-starred fish shack down the road and the extremely rare species of tree frog that lives on their property. *"No way, only ten in the world, wow, that's amazing."* See, it's easy.

You've no doubt done your research and read about ruins or gardens or a famous monument on the island. That's great, but you will never see any of them. At first, you'll feel a bit guilty about not *learning* anything while visiting and mention maybe doing a little cultural sightseeing.

However, you'll soon admit to yourself that won't happen because of your host's lack of enthusiasm, paired with your own realization that failure to visit the remains of an old battleship won't make you a terrible person. Plus, it would interfere with another activity that usually takes precedent over everything else when you're a tropical houseguest: drinking.

Your host invited you to this remote paradise, as they viewed you as someone who would not judge and hopefully join in their frequent consumption of alcohol. Island life mentality allows for day drinking, night drinking, beach drinking, drinking on a bike, right-after-you-brush-your-teeth drinking—basically, whenever you feel like having a drink, it's allowed. So if you'd frown upon seeing someone drinking a rum punch with their morning omelet, maybe rethink whether island life is for you. Being labeled a buzzkill by your host is the *worst*, and you wouldn't have any fun hanging out with people you consider a bunch of drunks. Changes in latitudes, changes in attitudes.

Since you're in a remote location, there's not a lot to do (see: drinking), so you'll end up spending a lot of time at the house. Make sure to bring books and download anything you might want to watch or listen to, as there's a good chance that Wi-Fi will be spotty or nonexistent. Also, island life is about getting away from it all, so don't be the guest who's constantly on your phone making business calls. Forcing others to listen to any phone call that includes the words "paradigm shift," "synergy," or "circle back" should be punishable by law.

When you're in a tropical paradise, the real world seems light-years away, and you'll feel as if anything goes. However, just because you see thatched roofs and monkeys in the trees doesn't mean there aren't laws you have to follow. You're in another country with a whole new set of rules, and if you break those rules, they have these places called jails with big, scary guards and inmates. Watch a couple episodes of *Locked Up Abroad* before your next tropical trip. You'll no longer think it might be fun to score an illegal substance or break into a temple, as you don't want to be the houseguest who had to stay behind for three to five years.

While not breaking any *actual* laws, there is some conduct the island houseguest should keep in mind. For instance, wear clothes. After being poolside or at the beach, cover up. Nobody wants to look at your sweaty, stinky, sunburned body as you chomp on a tortilla chip, dropping crumbs into the folds of your stomach. If by chance there's a "clothing-optional" beach, you should opt for clothes. Everybody has a camera, probably even the monkeys, so you and your privates could easily end up a meme.

Just because you're far away from home does not suddenly make you a new person. Yes, island life is more relaxed and carefree, but that does not open the door for such head-scratchingly odd behaviors as braiding and beading your hair, never wearing shoes, or adopting a weird way of speaking that sounds like Bob Marley meets Gillian Anderson's Margaret Thatcher. Using local expressions is clever for the first three hundred times you do it and then quickly moves to the category of "Please, please, stop!"

When dealing with locals, there's a fine line between friendly and patronizing. The guy renting you a bicycle doesn't want to be your best friend, and the bartender at the marina doesn't need to do a shot with you. It's great to tip well, but don't present it in a way that makes it seem like you think you're changing their life.

Be aware that music is something that can oddly cause friction when you're an island houseguest. The host likes to set the mood for the place, and that mood is often created by the music they choose. So before changing the music that's playing, always check with your host to see if it's OK. Granted, three hours of Jack Johnson could put anyone in a coma, but get the go-ahead from your host before putting on something else. That way, you'll be thought of as a thoughtful houseguest versus the jerk who hates Jack Johnson.

CHAPTER 8

THE REVIEWS ARE IN

The Airbnb Houseguest

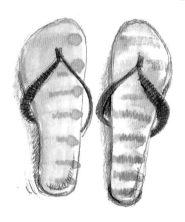

There's a great scene in the movie *Flirting with Disaster* where the proprietor of an excruciatingly twee bed-and-breakfast screams, "You are NOT B&B people!" at Ben Stiller. This also applies to Airbnbs. Some people love the idea of staying at someone else's home, while others find it creepy. The only way to know whether you are "Airbnb people" is to give it a try and see if it works for you. A-frames, split-levels, tree houses, lofts—you can find most every type of place to stay on Airbnb, and though you're paying money to stay there, you are still basically a houseguest in someone else's home.

If you do give Airbnb a try, finding the right place can be tricky. When you first go to the Airbnb website, you are dazzled by all the pretty pictures and intriguing headlines. You get all excited and want to start packing immediately and think if you don't book that "one-of-a-kind artistic houseboat" NOW, you'll have no place to stay. Relax! Don't book the first thing you see, because there will always be another place. Plus, once you pay, getting a refund if you cancel is a hassle, so take your time. You should also definitely *read the reviews*. Most guests give positive reviews, so if someone takes the time to write a detailed bad review, you should probably look for somewhere else. Sure, there might be a negative review from someone with a petty complaint ("the birds in the morning were very loud"), but you can usually sort those from the ones with a real grievance.

Look closely at the photos that accompany the listings. Pretend it's CSI: Airbnb and search for clues and look for anything that seems odd. "Why is that toilet next to the stove?" "Is that barbed wire on the windows?" "Do those polka dots on the bedspread have legs . . . and antennae?" Hosts try to sell their listing with the photos, so if the place doesn't look good in photos, it will look a lot worse in person. You want a place with the least amount of clutter possible. An antique bird cage collection might seem charming, but it will lose its allure when you trip over it in the middle of the night when heading to the bathroom. Clutter also means hard to clean, so search for a place that isn't jam-packed with stuff. Also, look for the basics in photos: make sure that the bathroom isn't gross and that the bed is a *real bed*, not a sofa bed, unless you enjoy pinching your fingers in a metal hinge. Also, before you book, ask the host questions like how strong the Wi-Fi signal is and whether there's currently any construction in the area. Showing up to a place with loin-vibrating jackhammering outside your window isn't fun. If the host doesn't reply to your questions in forty-eight hours, that's a sign the place isn't for you.

As you read the Airbnb listings, you quickly realize that some words seem to be code for other things. Unique = really weird layout; bohemian

= dirty; authentic = seven flights of stairs; cozy = you'll definitely whack your head on the ceiling. More unusual places like yurts or houses made from cargo containers seem cool in theory, but once you're staying there, you'll find yourself saying, "I'll never trust photos again." It's smart to go with more traditional places that offer fewer surprises. Bragging about sleeping in an igloo would get old anyway.

Location is another thing to be careful about when looking for an Airbnb. If you type in the name of a city, tons of places will show up in your search, but they could be far from where you want to be. Generally, the cheaper the place is, the farther away it is from the action. While a listing may say New Orleans, you could end up staying way out in the bayou, surrounded by alligators and wondering where all the drunk people with beads are. Always double-check the map that shows where the places are located and, again, READ THE REVIEWS.

Airbnb has certain hosts who are designated as Superhosts. These are the cool kids of Airbnb who have a history of five-star ratings and glowing reviews. Be sure to look for Superhosts, as they are serious about hosting and make the extra effort. Non-Superhosts are usually just starting out hosting or have not received the best reviews; they also are more likely to cancel your reservation after it's booked. You can also search the reviews for keywords like "problem," "unhappy," and "Ted Bundy."

When Airbnb-ing, you can decide what kind of experience you want. One way is to stay at the host's home while they are staying there as well. Some people find this an interesting way to meet locals and get an insider's perspective on the area they're visiting. Others would rather be drawn and quartered than stay with a stranger. The notion that you would pay money to sleep under the same roof with someone you don't know, be forced to make small talk, and—dare I type it—share a bathroom is more than one person's worst nightmare. Yes, it's totally possible you could stay with really great people who keep out of your way and add a lot

THINGS FOUND
after house guest

LOS ANGELES

Melted cup of Pinkberry.

LA County Parking Ticket.

Napkin with phone number of guy claiming to be a Hemsworth.

NEW ORLEANS

Tangled ball of Mardi Gras beads.

Broken high-heel shoe.

Empty bottle of Pepto-Bismol.

LONDON

Bag of Walker's Cheese and Onion crisps.

Pub coasters.

Tags from fake Burberry scarf from Portobello road.

BURRRRBERRY

MIAMI

FAENA

Glitter press-on nail.
Publix sub wrapper.
Matches from Faena Hotel.

IN GUEST ROOM
leaves, by city

TOKYO

Golf tees.
Hello Kitty condoms.

SEATTLE

Banjo pick.
Nordstrom shopping Bag.
Beard trimmings.

NEW YORK

Dear Evan Hansen playbill.

Half an Everything Bagel.

Tags from fake michael Kors
bag bought on Canal street.

PARIS

Three loose Gauloises.
Leaf from Luxembourg Gardens.
Unread copy of Proust.

to your visit, and there's also a chance you could be walking into a Norman Bates–lite situation. Staying somewhere that gives you the heebie-jeebies (medical term), even for a couple nights, isn't worth it. If you get to the point during your Airbnb stay where you ask yourself "Should I leave?" . . . leave. Always leave.

If staying at an Airbnb where the host is not in da house, remember this is someone's home and don't do anything you wouldn't do at your own place. Would you leave wet towels on hardwood floors or do that thing where you lean back on a chair and balance it on two legs? Well, then don't do it at an Airbnb either.

At a self-check-in Airbnb, with no one there to greet you upon arrival, make sure to TRIPLE-, no, QUADRUPLE-check the procedure to get the keys to the place. If you're lucky, there might be a super or property manager to let you in, but most absent hosts use lockboxes with combinations to deliver the keys. Make sure the host gives you the correct combination and ask if there is anything tricky about using the lockbox or keys. Check whether you need to jiggle, pull, or push anything. Also, get detailed instructions as to where the lockbox is located, because many times they're hard to find. The host might say "the lockbox is near the garage," which is zero help when you're searching in the dark. It's much better to be a little annoying and pester for specifics than to stand in the rain with your luggage and no way inside.

Your Airbnb is not a hotel, so don't be surprised if the bedding isn't a zillion thread count and the decor screams IKEA. You are usually paying less than a hotel for more space, and you have a kitchen to cook in, so deal with the Garfield sheets.

CHAPTER 9

DESPERATE HOUSEGUESTS

How Low Will You Go for a Free Place to Stay?

You want to go to Florence and Amsterdam, and you still need to see the polar bears in Alaska, and when it gets cold, the Bahamas sound amazing. There's just one problem: your bank account is shaking its head NO. There are times when your travel plans far exceed your travel funds, and instead of giving up and staying home, you need to do whatever it takes to make your travel dreams come true. This means being a houseguest at places you usually wouldn't want to stay. You sit at your computer with your finger poised over the send button as you debate whether you really want to ask your name-dropping cousin who threw pine cones at you as a kid whether you can stay with him. Then you remember his place in Montauk is right on the beach and say "What the hell" and hit send.

As a houseguest, there are some things to consider when you have the itch to travel but don't have the scratch to finance it.

REMEMBER ME?

Throughout life you meet a lot of people. Some you spend a lot of time with, and others you share just a few fleeting moments. However, these are meaningful moments at a bar, as seatmates on a plane, or at the "fun table" at a wedding, where you promise to absolutely, positively keep in touch. Now is the time to show that you take promises seriously and that you have zero shame when it comes to finding a free place to stay. It's probably wise to text your one-time new best friend when getting reacquainted versus calling or emailing. They may not open an email from someone whose name they don't recognize, and a phone call would be too uncomfortable for everyone. A text shows you thought enough of them to keep their number in your phone, and if they've deleted you, you quickly have the upper hand. Once you get the "Who dis?" part out of the way, do a few days of chatting before approaching the topic of visiting. If they invite you to be a houseguest, do not play the old "I wouldn't want to impose" routine. They might not offer again, so accept instantly. Also, be aware that once you stay with this person, you have opened up the concept of houseguest reciprocity, so don't be surprised if they soon ask to stay at your place. Quid pro quo, Clarice, quid pro quo.

TOTO, WE'RE NOT AT THE RITZ CARLTON ANYMORE

If you're worried and can't sleep, just count the roaches instead of sheep. You've accepted your host's invitation knowing that the accommodations won't exactly be first class. However, they were nice enough to let you stay, so if you accept their invitation, you CANNOT complain, judge, gasp in horror, roll your eyes, exclaim "Oh my God, there's a dirty litter box next to this air mattress," or display any reaction that suggests you are freaked out by your surroundings. Where you're staying may have mold in the shower and a subway train right outside the window, but it's also someone's home, and they love it, and since you are staying there for free, you're in no position to be snooty. Be as appreciative as you would be if staying at an amazing beach house in St. Bart's. OK, bad example. You'd donate a kidney to get asked back to St. Bart's, so be as appreciative as you would be if staying at a friend's place that doesn't have a leaking air conditioner that sounds like a freight train and is propped up with LEGO blocks.

Your host no doubt realizes their place isn't five-star, so if they apologize about its lack of luxury, it is important you remain gracious. Try to remember everything you learned in that one drama course you took because that guy who looked like Channing Tatum was taking it and ACT as if everything is great. Point out something positive, like the good pizza place around the corner or how close it is to the park. Not being a dick feels good.

You are allowed to leave a host's place if it's so bad that you think your personal safety is at risk. A faulty furnace, a stairwell littered with hypodermic needles, or anything else that could lead to a headline that includes the words "death trap" means get the hell out of there.

PLANES, TRAINS, AND POSSIBLY AN AUTOMOBILE

You're dying to see that show at the Met but need a place to stay in New York City. You might be lucky enough to have a friend with a two-bedroom duplex in Tribeca who leaves the keys with the doorman and tells you to have a good time. Most likely, that's not going to happen. Yes, you do have a friend in New York . . . but not in Manhattan, or Brooklyn, or Queens, or whatever those other boroughs are. Your friend lives about two hours from New York City, and if you stay with them, some serious schlepping will be involved to see that Met show.

How far a host's place is from where you want to be is something a houseguest needs to think about. Any place under an hour commute is fine, but if you're stuck way out in the boondocks, you'll spend most of your time traveling back and forth and won't get a true sense of the place you're visiting. If you flew in for the weekend to soak up the flavor of Miami but end up in the suburbs going to the Cheesecake Factory and outlet malls, what's the point? You might want to delay your trip until you can afford to stay somewhere closer to the center of things . . . or make a new friend with a killer place in South Beach.

SLEEPING WITH THE FRENEMY

You ended your relationship on really good terms. You got the NutriBullet juicer, and they kept all the vinyl, so being a houseguest with your ex should be perfectly fine. Maybe. When you break up with someone and don't completely hate one another, it's fine to run into each other at Whole Foods without any drama, but staying under the same roof is a different story. Various factors should influence your decision as to whether being a houseguest at your ex's place is a good or really, really, really bad idea.

If your ex is in a new relationship, it's unlikely this new person will be excited to see your underwear hanging in the bathroom of their current partner. Of course, you're both mature adults and can be civil to each other, but when you accidentally use their favorite coffee mug, they may be smiling, but their eyes are saying "What the hell are you doing in my kitchen?" If you do decide to stay with an ex, be prepared for a barrage of questions from everyone in your universe: your friends, your ex's friends, your mother, the UPS guy—they'll all want to know what's *really* going on between you two.

You should be careful that asking to stay at your ex's place isn't misconstrued as a sign you want to rekindle things. What you thought could be a fun weekend of reminiscing could quickly deteriorate into smashed plates and your host screaming, "Then WHY are you here? I thought you still loved me!"

Expectations could get complicated, especially when it comes to sleeping arrangements. If you arrive assuming you'd be sleeping on the sofa but quickly realize that your host has other ideas, do you need to worry that you'll be put out on the street if you don't, um, "cooperate"? Conversely, if you thought your stay was going to include pillow talk but are instantly shut down, do not act offended or try to discuss the matter. This could open up several cans of worms, Pandora's box, and a lot of other things that are best kept closed.

SOMETHING WICKED THIS WAY CRAWLS

If it were possible to put a siren and blinking warning lights in a book, they would go here. That's because when you're a houseguest, there is nothing you need to avoid more than this one word: **BEDBUGS**. If you have ever experienced the pure horror of bedbugs, you will understand the need for all caps and bold. Your host's home doesn't need to be dirty for these bloodsucking monsters to thrive, but they are harder to spot in a place that is messy or dirty. One of the most insidious things about bedbugs is that you may not see them and their bites may not appear for a few days. You may already be home from your trip before you realize they bit you. So during your stay, be on alert and check the seams of your mattress for any bugs or tiny black dots (bedbug poop, ugh). If you spot any sign of bedbugs, you should leave. Your host is probably not aware they have a problem, and if you choose to tell them, they may not love hearing the news, so be very careful how you inform them.

To avoid bringing these very tiny vampires home with you, never put your luggage on the floor or on the bed during your stay. Place luggage on a chair, on a dresser, or in the bathtub if possible—it sounds weird, but you're more likely to see them that way. Bedbugs climb into your luggage, and if they hitch a ride, getting rid of them is a long, painful, expensive process. Bedbug bites leave painful, scratchy welts. They also burrow into your psyche, causing insomnia, nightmares, and anxiety. If you think this is an exaggeration, go on YouTube and listen to people tell bedbug stories that are more terrifying than any sewer-side chat with Pennywise the clown. Bedbugs can live for a year without feeding, so even when you think they're gone for good, they're not. There are actual bedbug support groups, and people report PTSD from bedbug encounters. When you're a houseguest, you cannot be too vigilant in your efforts to avoid them. Bedbugs are one of the worst things you'll ever experience—yes, even worse than a day at the DMV and that three-and-a-half-hour performance of *Riverdance*.

CHAPTER 10

I'M SO FANCY
Staying with Rich People

"The rich are different." It was either F. Scott Fitzgerald or the Countess Luann who said that, and in some ways it's true. Not that the rich are better than anyone else; it's simply that how they operate is a bit different from how most people live.

In regard to the word "rich," let's define our terms. We're not talking owning-a-few-car-dealerships-in-St.-Louis rich here. By rich, we mean being *on*, or at least being *adjacent to*, the Forbes 400 list of richest people. The money could be inherited, the result of financial wizardry, or the windfall of some random invention (yes, there's a Spanx billionaire). It doesn't matter where all this cash came from; there just needs to be boat-loads of it to qualify as the kind of rich that is commonly called "Oprah money." Your college roommate is definitely crushing it with his ortho-dontia practice, but that's not the kind of rich that impacts the stock market, influences foreign governments, and gets you subpoenaed to testify before at least one really mean Senate subcommittee.

Depending on the type of rich locale you're invited to, your houseguest experience may vary. Here are some things to be aware of when staying with the haves and the have-mores.

DOWNTON SHABBY CHIC

This is usually an older home or historic house, and it will probably have a name instead of an address. Yes, it's a little pretentious naming a house, but if it was done two hundred years ago, there's no point in throwing shade at dead people. However, if the house is brand new and given a name, some eye-rolling is allowed. The newer the house, the more likely the name will be *everywhere*: on towels, napkins, glasses, ice buckets, and coasters as well as carved into stone at the driveway entrance or incorporated into the metalwork of a gate. At least you will never forget where you are. Plus, if by chance any items from the house are lost in a hurricane or nor'easter, those in the area will immediately know to return them to Thistlebriar, Larksthroat, or Squirrelsmead. Never ask about the house name's origin, as your host will either think you're judging them or bore you with a really long story that forces you to half smile for a half hour as they talk.

If the house is older, don't be surprised if it's not in the best shape or smells a little funky. The legitimately rich make little effort to impress others and see no reason to update anything in the house. Rugs are threadbare, chair cushion springs poke through, and dog hair abounds . . . even if there's no dog. A caretaker who has worked at the house for about a thousand years is often seen roaming the grounds. He will not like you, so there's no need to chat him up. You may get a strong *Wuthering Heights* vibe and be convinced you heard someone in the attic, because you probably did. Random relatives pop out of nowhere in places like this.

A LIL' YACHTY

The only person who could call a boat a yacht without sounding like a jerk was Thurston Howell III. (How did he and Lovey have so many wardrobe options on that island?) Even if it's seventy-plus feet, call it a boat. If you heard yourself say "I've had enough beach time for today; I'm going back to the yacht," you'd cringe. Some boats can be massive, with multiple floors, screening rooms, bars, pools, and a labyrinth of bedrooms, and though they are huge, they are still on the water, so pack Dramamine or those cool seasickness wristbands.

When you're a houseguest on a ginormous megayacht (very big boat), you are still in confined quarters, so going a bit buggy isn't uncommon. To avoid cabin fever, stay out on deck as much as possible. Also, since space is limited even on the biggest boats, you might be assigned a roommate. Don't be weird about it; don't hog the closets and make sure to give your roomie some time alone.

Yachts have crews who run the boat and are there to help you have a great time, including making drinks, serving food, etc. They are not employed to be flirted with. Any hanky and/or panky with the crew is really bad form, and getting a lecture from your host would be super demoralizing. Remember to tip the crew too: bring cash, as there are no ATMs at sea.

BOUND FOR THE COMPOUND

In addition to handsome people, touch football, and fun nicknames, the Kennedys can also be credited with making popular the concept of the rich hosting guests at a compound. Their family compound on Cape Cod has hosted everyone from Taylor Swift to Arnold the Governor/Terminator, who undoubtedly did not need help cracking open his lobster. "I am not a fan of za green stuff."

Compounds are basically a number of buildings spread over one piece of property, often passed down through families. There's usually a large main house with some smaller outbuildings as well as a pool house and sometimes a bunkhouse where the kids sleep and teenagers hide their bongs. The host and all guests at the compound usually get together for meals, and that's when houseguests often encounter compound traditions. These traditions could be anything from having to run around your chair three times if you use foul language to having to wear a court jester hat if it's your birthday. Sure, it's all weird and cultlike, but you must embrace these customs, and any unwillingness to do so will not be looked upon favorably. Hosts take this kind of stuff more seriously than you'd imagine, and you don't want to be blamed for bringing bad juju into the compound or stirring up some ancient family curse. So put on the damn hat; it's not going to kill you.

DOWN ON "THE FARM"

Rich people like to call something that is nothing like a farm, a farm. So if you are invited to be a houseguest at "the farm," don't expect to see fields of wheat and a rusty John Deere tractor. You're not dealing with *The Grapes of Wrath* here. If there are chickens, they will be some exotic variety of chicken with colorful plumage and a Ziggy Stardust haircut and live in charming little houses, not scary warehouses. Cattle could make an appearance, too, but they're ornamental and function more as moving sculptures versus future porterhouse steaks.

Don't be surprised if where you're sleeping is a repurposed something; maybe it was once a barn, a stable, or a silo. This use of these former farm structures lends cred to the whole agrarian gestalt, and if ever challenged as to the authenticity of their farm, the host need only point out that guests are sleeping in horse stalls.

Since it's called a "farm," your host feels obligated to put something in the ground besides a solar-heated swimming pool. Flower gardens are popular, as are more refined vegetables that look pretty growing in rows. Say something positive to your host about their farming ability so they don't think you view them as a dilettante in a totally spotless Carhartt jacket. They might also make small batches of artisanal cheese or honey from their very own bee apiary. If that's the case, commend them on their efforts to help the bees. Your host will be thrilled to be recognized as someone who helps the bees—everybody loves the bees! Their honey is often sold at local gourmet shops with the proceeds going to a local charity. It's a great way for your host to show they're supportive of the community and make points with the townsfolk when they try to build a twelve-foot-tall privacy fence that breaks every building code in the book.

RANCH DRESSING

Do you like chandeliers made out of antlers, Navajo blanket dog beds, and guys who've never been on a horse who wear cowboy hats? Well, then you're in for a treat if you're a houseguest at a rich person ranch. Rich people ranches are located in some of the most beautiful areas of the country, which are usually very remote; in fact, the harder the place is to get to, the more desirable it is to your host. Make sure you mention you realize how remote their place is and your host will silently thank you, as you just gave them an opportunity to "chopper-drop" and retell their story about that time they landed their Sikorsky in a cow pasture. "Then the bull started to charge us!" Your host is spending a lot of money to live out their Dutton family fantasy, and if you accept an invitation, you must show great restraint and ignore any new ridiculous "ranchy" behaviors your host may exhibit. These may include wearing a lot of turquoise, chewing tobacco, and giving their vintage Land Rover a human name.

The television show *Yellowstone* has added to the proliferation of rich people ranches. In fact, many celebrities now own fancy ranches, as they offer an escape from the limelight and massive tax breaks (we see you, Wyoming). If you should encounter any celebrities while you're a ranch houseguest, treat them like you would anyone else. No staring, no pointing, and *definitely* no photos. However, you may text your friends back home to say, "I just saw David Letterman buying beef jerky."

HORSE PLAY

—James S., Millbrook, New York

Staying at a fancy country estate in Virginia is probably the closest an American can get to a *Downton Abbey* British fantasy without boarding a plane or stealing a corgi. So as someone who went as zombie Maggie Smith for Halloween, I was thrilled to be invited to my friend Brooke's fortieth birthday weekend at her family's grand home in Middleburg. Middleburg is a painfully adorable town in the Blue Ridge Mountains. However, this isn't your typical backwoods whistle-stop. This is a place where price-gouging gourmet stores abound (why is this egg salad fourteen dollars?) and where you can probably find a drive-through cashmere shop. Think of it as the Hamptons with no ocean and a Southern accent.

Middleburg is also the heart of horse country, meaning if you ride, breed, board, groom, or remotely care about large four-legged animals that eat hay, it's the place to be. It's not uncommon to see people walking around town in riding boots and jodhpurs or wearing one of those bright red jackets with a velvet collar that make you look like you jumped off a Johnnie Walker bottle. I had no problem with horses, as evidenced by the fact that I recently rooted for the pony on *The Masked Singer*. This was a good thing, as the birthday weekend had a definite horse theme. Each guest room was assigned the name of a different breed of horse: Appaloosa, Arabian, Morgan. I was in the Friesian room, a breed I learned only comes in black and is popular with little Dutch girls and the Third Horseman of the Apocalypse. In my room, I found a horse's feed bag that served as a gift bag for the weekend guests. Inside were fancy body lotions, a horse hair hairbrush, a soy candle that smelled like a horse barn, and elegantly decorated cookies shaped like different famous horses. As I sat on my bed, munching on Secretariat, I realized a couple things: my hosts were not messing around when it came to a party theme, and my fellow houseguests were serious or at least competent riders. I, on the other hand, had ridden a horse three times in my life, one of those times being when I was six at a petting zoo at a mall in Sandusky, Ohio. I think Brooke assumed I rode because of my Prince Charles–casual wardrobe. I was into lots of tattersall checked shirts and heavy briar-resistant tweeds back then, but I drew a line at wearing a kilt.

Because of my lack of equestrian skills, I thought I could dodge all riding outings by being extremely helpful to Brooke's parents. I set up the bar, moved garden furniture, and took their French bulldog on so many exhausting walks it started to hide when it saw me.

The day of the actual birthday was to kick off with a foxhunt in the morning. Yes, that's right, everyone would be looking for a fox on horseback. However, no foxes would be harmed during this hunt. It was more about dressing up, blowing a horn, and riding around the countryside yelling "Tallyho." A fox would be tracked using its footprints and poop (it's pointy and full of berries, if curious), and once we saw the fox, we got to eat lunch and drink Bloody Marys. Everyone would be going on the hunt, including the birthday girl's father, who would lead it, so there was no getting out of it. I just had to hold on till we got to the Bloody Marys.

I knew choosing the right horse would hugely impact my ride. I didn't want some horse with Triple Crown aspirations. I needed a horse with nothing to prove: a horse that was happy to graze and swat the occasional fly and completely fine with carrying a human on its back. I found that horse in Linda, a dark gray mare. Linda had a pleasant "sure, whatever" demeanor and did exactly what was asked of her. Before going with Linda, I grilled a stable hand about the horses, making sure to avoid any animal described as "complicated," "mercurial," or "never the same since that lightning strike."

I managed to get on the horse without too much difficulty. I didn't plan on being a speed demon or doing any trick moves; my goal was just to stay upright. If I kept at a steady, controlled pace and Linda continued to cooperate, things would be fine.

We had been riding for about an hour when there was some excitement about fresh fox tracks. The other riders picked up their pace in pursuit of the fox, but I was content staying at the relaxed trot I'd established with Linda. I was proud that she didn't race ahead to be with the pack. Linda didn't need group approval; she was definitely her own horse.

After a few minutes, I lost sight of the others and thought maybe I should go a tiny bit faster. I didn't want to be the houseguest they had to send out a search party for. I indicated to Linda that I was ready to move from a trot to a slightly faster trot, and she obliged. Maybe I was an equestrian after all and not just a guy with a lot of tweed jackets!

The group had stopped in a clearing up ahead. Linda came to a halt, and I waved to them and they waved back. I felt rather self-satisfied sitting upon my cooperative steed. Then . . . I fell. I wish I could say a rattlesnake spooked the horse or I attempted to jump a wall, but none of that happened. For absolutely no reason whatsoever, I toppled from my horse and hit the ground hard.

Brooke and the other riders quickly came over to see whether I was all right, and the short answer was no. My shoulder felt like it was on backward, and even the slightest movement was excruciating. Linda looked down at me but passed no judgment. There was talk of an ambulance, but I quickly kiboshed that knowing my fall could end up in the local paper with the headline "Overdressed Houseguest Ruins Birthday Weekend."

I was strapped in to the rear seat of a golf cart and driven back to the house by Brooke's college-aged brother. He offered to "do a bowl" with me to help with the pain, but I declined. When I removed my shirt and looked in the mirror, I could instantly tell something was wrong. My one shoulder was square, like a badly drawn robot. I was taken to the local emergency room, where I met with a chatty doctor who looked like Pat Sajak. He told me I had dislocated my shoulder and possibly torn my rotator cuff (an ultrasound later confirmed it). I couldn't believe I had done this much damage while standing still on a horse, but Pat Sajak assured me this was very common and outlined, in horrific detail, other horse-related injuries he'd witnessed. As he talked, he nonchalantly popped my shoulder back in place without any warning. I assumed I'd be given a stick to bite down on, or told to brace myself like they do on airplanes before a crash landing, but no. And, oh yes, I screamed.

I left the ER wearing my new shoulder sling and carrying a bottle of rather large pain pills—pills that ironically could have been described as big enough to choke a horse. I apologized in every way possible to my hosts and planned on immediately heading back home, but they insisted that I stay for the black-tie birthday dinner that evening.

The rest of the day I spent on the sofa drifting in and out of sleep. I had some bizarre dreams thanks to the medication; one featured characters from *The Wizard of Oz*. Was I Dorothy? Was Pat Sajak the Tin Man? Was Linda the Good Witch or the Bad Witch? No man knows.

It never occurred to me just how much you need your shoulder to do simple tasks until I tried to get dressed that evening. Buttoning my shirt was impossible, and tying a bow tie, even when not loopy on pain pills, is a Rubik's Cube–ish brain fuck. Thus, I was forced to enlist the help of my fellow houseguests. I had four people fussing over me, each with strong opinions on how to dress a grown man. They were like the mice in *Cinderella* preparing me for the ball. I didn't know these people very well, yet I was perfectly fine letting them shove their hands down my pants to make me presentable. The kept talking as if I wasn't in the room, saying things like, "If his neck wasn't so thick, this would be easier" and "No, that's not a lump in the fabric; it's his stomach." Once dressed and seated at the dinner table, I managed to feed myself, which I felt was a major accomplishment. Though cutting my meat required assistance from my dinner partner, who also had to wipe the mouth of the tuxedo-wearing toddler next to her.

I did everything I could not to be a downer houseguest and ruin the party. I had a glass of champagne but didn't overdo it, as I knew mixing alcohol with pills could take the evening in a whole new direction. I even danced a little, though I did not compete in the midnight limbo competition.

I ended up sleeping in the tuxedo, as it was easier than having strangers put their hands in my pants again. I fashioned a metal coat hanger and some Velcro into a device I used to pick things up and close zippers. I would use this device for the next couple months while I recovered. I often wonder whether I missed out on a huge business opportunity by not marketing this device. If it ever shows up on *Shark Tank*, I'll be crushed.

As I prepared to leave the next morning, I saw Linda in the meadow behind the barn. I thought I should at least say goodbye and walked over toward her. She looked at me and then slowly walked to where I was standing. Wow, she remembered me and maybe was even worried about me, I thought. This could be a *Gorillas in the Mist* moment, when man and beast have a strong unspoken connection. She then lunged for the corn muffin in my hand.

CHAPTER 11

A ROOM HOPEFULLY WITH A VIEW

The Hotel Houseguest

There's nothing better than staying at a good hotel. Who cares if the Toblerone in the minibar is fifteen dollars; if it wasn't for hotels, you probably would never have learned about Toblerone . . . delicious triangular Swiss chocolate—tell me more! Staying at a hotel is glamorous, exciting, and probably the closest you'll ever get to feeling like James Bond. Unless, of course, you're Daniel Craig reading this, and if so, we forgive you for *Cowboys & Aliens*, and please do more films like *Layer Cake*. One of the best things about staying at a hotel is that nobody knows you; you are completely anonymous and can adopt whatever persona you wish. While sitting at a hotel bar, talking to strangers, you can become 007 in Dockers or anyone else you choose to be. Chances are those you're talking to are also embellishing things a bit as well. Who knew one hotel bar could be home to so many tech billionaires, former Olympians, and ex-girlfriends of Leo DiCaprio?

When you're staying at a hotel, you're technically not a houseguest, but you are a guest nonetheless, so there are ways to properly behave, just as there are when staying with a friend. This is the only time people are actually paid to ensure your guest experience is as flawless as possible. When you check in to any fairly good hotel, most times the people you deal with went to school for hospitality and hotel management. They aren't just doing this as some temp job till they join the road company of *Les Miz*. They choose a career focused on taking care of people while they're away from home. They're genuinely concerned about the water pressure in your shower and want you to be happy with the view from your room. If you aren't, they want to know about it. However, you can let them know in a way that doesn't immediately put you in the category of whiny asshat. Yelling at a front desk person about how loud the pigeons are outside your window or being outraged at the fact the hotel doesn't get the Disney Channel is pointless. If you throw a hotel tantrum, you're guaranteed to feel like a jerk later, and you'll be forced to dodge that desk person for the rest of your stay. Instead, first vent your problem to someone you know. Once you say it out loud, you'll realize how *Real Housewives*-ish you sound and will either abandon the idea of complaining or do so in a rational manner.

Most good hotels also have a concierge. This is a person with a hard-to-pronounce job title who can do a lot to help guests get the most out of their stay. If you think you'll need help with dinner reservations, renting cars, or getting tickets to plays, concerts, etc., it's wise to introduce yourself to the concierge when you arrive. A good concierge can work magic, as they have connections with the best restaurants and ticket brokers in the city. They can probably arrange tickets to *Hamilton* if you're willing to pay top dollar, but they can't get you front-row seats next to Drake at the Grammys. Don't be put out if they are honest with you about next-to-impossible requests. A concierge can find non-crazy-people babysitters, send flowers, and arrange hair appointments and are thrilled when they can help guests out. However, hooking you up with a weed dealer or finding you a "date" is not part of their job description. You should also tip them accordingly, up front, depending on how much help you think you'll need. If handing people money makes you at all squeamish, put cash, along with a brief note, in an envelope with the concierge's name and leave it at the desk. A few Andrew Jacksons will do nicely as an introduction and guarantee the concierge will be happy to make a few calls on your behalf.

Yes, you are paying a fair amount of money for your room, but that does not give you carte blanche to turn it into a toxic waste dump. The housekeeping staff is there to keep things tidy, change the linens, and do light cleaning; they aren't a hazmat unit. Leave the room close to how your bedroom looks at home. Would you toss the remains of a late-night Taco Bell run on your bedroom floor at home? Then put it in the trash, and if you order room service, place the dishes and tray in the hallway. Also, while you don't need to keep the bathroom spotless, it shouldn't scream *Forensic Files* either. If your room isn't cleaned by early afternoon, you should let management know. However, housekeepers are usually eager to get into your room and get their work done early, so remember to take the "Do Not Disturb" sign off your door; otherwise, you may go to the end of the queue. It's a magical feeling returning to your room after a long day out to find your bed turned down, your clothes folded, and fresh towels waiting for you. It's like elves came in while you were out and made everything perfect. Housekeepers do a thankless job, so if you see them, say thank you, and tip them **well**, especially if your company is paying for your room. Bury it in your taxi receipts. Hey, if you can hide four Moscow mules, you can hide a housekeeping tip.

While the front desk staff and concierge are incredibly good at recommendations of multistar restaurants and other top-drawer activities, sometimes while traveling you're looking for places that are a bit more unconventional. If you want secret dive bars, a drag show taco joint, or mildly dangerous afterhours clubs, some great resources are the valet guys who park your car. For some reason, valet guys always seem to know the wildest places and never steer you wrong. If your hotel doesn't have valet, consult the hotel bartender; they are also experts at veering you in the direction of local trouble. Ask around a bit and, next thing you know, it's 5:00 a.m. and you're in some club you entered via a door behind a dumpster.

Many seem confused about what you call it when you take items from a hotel room that don't belong to you. Well, it's called stealing, and don't do it. Things such as soap, shampoo, disposable slippers, packets of coffee, hotel stationery and pens, and anything the hotel clearly marks as complimentary are totally fine to put in your luggage. However, pillows, blankets, silverware, paintings (yup, people steal them), china, and basically anything with an electrical cord should remain in the room. You may fall in love with the big, fluffy robe in the bathroom, but be aware: if it follows you home, you'll get billed for it. Though if you ask, they are usually available for sale. Two items where there's a *slight* gray area are towels and umbrellas. If the towels have the hotel name emblazoned on them, you're allowed to take **one** and **only one time**. You're not allowed to use the hotel as a resource to fill up your home linen closet, and you can take the towel only if it's very cool. Agreed, this is kind of a lame move, but in the scheme of things, it's not that horrible an offense. Similarly, if you have been using a heavily branded hotel umbrella, ask the staff if it's OK to take it home; they'll most likely say yes, as they buy them in bulk and it's free advertising for the hotel. Packing the umbrella in your luggage or getting one on an airplane could prove more trouble than it's worth, unless you're Mary Poppins. Wait, Mary Poppins wouldn't need an airplane, would she?

WE ALL DESERVE A BED-7

—Molly Shannon, Actress, Los Angeles

You've no doubt heard of 007, the Chicago Seven, and the Seven Wonders of the World, but you've probably never heard of a Bed-7. Well, get ready for a treat! A Bed-7 is my way to totally relax and let the pressures of the day just melt away. Surely, there are countless other ways to unwind, but I believe few involve a cheeseburger and mayonnaise.

I should probably clarify that a Bed-7 has no scientific basis, nor is it FDA approved or even Goop endorsed. A Bed-7 is something I created as a way to de-stress and let anything that is currently weighing you down disappear, even if only for a short time. Basically, to complete a Bed-7, you stay in bed for seven hours and remain wide awake while enjoying some of your favorite stress-free activities. However, to fully appreciate a Bed-7, there are some guidelines you should follow.

First, you need a bed, but, and this is important, you are not allowed to go to sleep. Not because of some Freddy Krueger thing but because you want to be fully conscious in order to enjoy every magical moment of your Bed-7. It can be executed anywhere, but I find a Bed-7 in a hotel room or a friend's guest room extra special. You emerge from the room renewed and refreshed, and the world seems full of promise. If you Bed-7 at home, you might emerge and realize you forgot the frozen pizza in the oven or still need to do laundry, so away from home is preferable.

The optimal hours for a Bed-7 are from 1:00 p.m. to 8:00 p.m., though that is not written in stone. Everything about the Bed-7 should be on your own terms, so if you decide to do an early-morning Bed-7, that is perfectly acceptable.

Propping yourself up in the bed with two large, cushy pillows is recommended. Or, even better, one of those cushioned bed chairs with arms that fabulous movie star ladies like Barbara Stanwyck used when sitting in bed. "Sorry, *wrong number*, sucker; I'm enjoying a Bed-7!"

Talking on the phone and email are *not* allowed during a Bed-7, though some light texting is permitted. I suggest keeping it to topics like what to buy your sister for her birthday or where you can get a really good Cobb salad. All business matters and drama-heavy issues have no place in a Bed-7.

During your Bed-7, you may watch television, but make sure your viewing choices are uncomplicated and pleasant. *The Repair Shop*, *90 Day Fiancé*, and any competition show featuring a host with an impressive sweater collection are recommend. Movies are allowed as well, but nothing anxiety inducing. A Bed-7 is about escaping all that. If the film features Diane Lane wearing linen on an island, you're headed in the right direction. And always remember to keep the remote close, because a frantic search for the remote can quickly derail a Bed-7.

Music is encouraged during a Bed-7, but nothing dark and brooding. I personally find show tunes to be perfect for a Bed-7. Singing along to the Broadway cast recording of *Oklahoma!*, *Hello, Dolly!*, *Mamma Mia!*, or any other musical with an exclamation point in its title will definitely add to your experience. Oh, what a beautiful morning it is . . . when you're fully immersed in a Bed-7!

Casual browsing of Amazon, Etsy, and eBay is fine, but proceed with caution. Getting embroiled in a heated bidding war over a Donald Duck cookie jar would create negative energy that takes your Bed-7 to places you don't want it to go.

Magazines and books are permitted too. *Entertainment Weekly*, *The New Yorker*, *Kinfolk*, and all home decor magazines that offer unexpected uses for sea glass are Bed-7 appropriate. Books that transport you to another world are great for a Bed-7, as are memoirs. I mean, reading about the day in 1967 when Mia Farrow got her revolutionary pixie hair cut that she debuted in the film *Rosemary's Baby*—could there be anything better? I think not.

Podcasts can be tricky. Many of my favorites feature curious crimes and murders, things you should shy away from during a Bed-7, so keep that in mind when selecting.

Food is a hugely important part of your seven-hour escape, and the official meal of a Bed-7 is a cheeseburger and fries with mayo on the side. I've experimented with other meals, but the burger and fries combo is definitely the way to go, as it's well suited for eating in bed. It also fits perfectly under those silver room service plate covers (see above: hotel room), making it seem like a magic trick when it's revealed—voilà! Feel free to substitute vegetarian burgers, but you must order fries; I will have to stand firm on this point. Unfortunately, snacks like chips, cookies, and popcorn are frowned upon during a Bed-7, as they leave crumbs and crumbs can lead to *bed stress*, something I'll cover in more depth at another time.

You should also experience your Bed-7 alone. Having a friend or significant other accompany you during a Bed-7 simply won't work. However, pets may join you on your Bed-7, as they seem to have a silent understanding of what you hope to achieve on your journey. Pets won't start talking about how they should really stop dating Jonathan or encourage you to cut your Bed-7 time short. A Bed-5? Sorry, that's not going to happen on my watch.

CHAPTER 12

HO, HO, HO, GUESS WHO'S COMING TO TOWN

Houseguests at the Holidays

Book early. No matter whether it's Memorial Day, Juneteenth, Washington's birthday, or any other holiday that brings with it a day off from work and a mattress sale, it's wise to let your host know as soon as possible that you'd like to visit. If you wait too long, you run the risk of being told there's no room at the inn, as holidays are high season for houseguests. When people look at their calendars and realize a holiday is nearing, they feel compelled to go somewhere, basically anywhere. There's a mad frenzy to get out of town, as they don't want to be left behind with the social lepers who are forced to sit home and look at the Instagram photos of their friends who had the foresight to book early.

If you do manage to snag a holiday invitation, remember the words of that great philosopher Madonna, who said, "Holiday. It would be. It would be so nice." To guarantee that your time as a holiday houseguest is as nice as possible, keep in mind the following:

FOURTH OF JULY

A holiday centered around pyrotechnics is admittedly a little bizarre. Yes, the Fourth of July is supposed to be about celebrating America's independence, but as you scarf down hot dogs and potato salad, it's far more likely you'll be discussing when to start blowing things up than liberation from British rule. The Fourth of July is one of the most popular holidays for houseguests, as it signals the start of summer travel season and the start of summer FOMO season, so people scramble to escape their homes and not miss the fun train. On the Fourth of July everyone is a flag waver, so if you're a houseguest on this holiday, leave your politics at the door. It's great that you read blogs and watch cable news shows and worked at your local polling place, but on Independence Day limit your opinions to whether baked beans should contain brown sugar (yes) and whether you have to follow the official rules of Wiffle Ball (no). Now go belly flop down a Slip 'N Slide, light a damn sparkler, and have fun.

HALLOWEEN

For some reason, people have rather strong opinions about Halloween. Either they're a thousand percent IN and can tell you the best pumpkin patch within a hundred miles and start making their costumes sometime in June or they're Halloween haters who work themselves into a frenzy at the mere mention of candy corn. Regardless of where your host falls on the Halloween love/hate spectrum, when you're a houseguest, you must happily go along with their position on the holiday. If you're staying with someone who watches *It's the Great Pumpkin, Charlie Brown* like they're studying the Zapruder film, they don't want to hear any negativity when it comes to one of their favorite days of the year. Similarly, if you're a houseguest in a Halloween-free home, don't show up at breakfast in a Shrek mask and badger your host for being "too cool" for a little Halloween fun.

If your host belongs to the first category, feel free to go batshit for bats, ghosts, wax vampire fangs, and Styrofoam tombstones and, sure, go ahead and pack your special jack-o'-lantern carving tool you bought at the dollar store. Your host will be thrilled to have a houseguest who enthusiastically joins them in covering their home with fake cobwebs that will be impossible to get rid of for about a year. If your host needs some help passing out candy to trick-or-treaters, offer to take over. After the sixth Thomas the Tank Engine at the door, they might need a break.

If your host is anti-Halloween, you may have to sit in the dark hiding from children ringing the doorbell in search of mini Snickers. If that does happen, the next day pretend you don't mind helping clean up the toilet paper hanging from their trees and bushes, left behind by the disappointed Snickers seekers.

THANKSGIVING

Whether your hosts are friends or family will impact your Thanksgiving houseguest experience. A family Thanksgiving is more about spending time together and catching up, while a Thanksgiving spent with friends is more about camaraderie. Not to say a family Thanksgiving can't be fun, but in addition to the cranberries and rolls that come in a tube, the turkey often comes with a side of anxiety (see: "You Can Go Home Again"). Holidays can be stressful, as people want everything to be perfect and lumpy gravy has caused more than one Thanksgiving host to totally lose their mind. One way to keep your Thanksgiving family visit from going off the rails is to keep the visit short—one or two nights at most. This is more than enough time to hear about who died, who's getting married, and who's on the wait list at Dartmouth. Then pack up your Tupperware full of leftovers and head out. If your hosts beg you to stay longer, blame traffic and your need to get on the road before things "get crazy out there."

If you're a houseguest with friends during Thanksgiving, bring **good** wine. If it's served at dinner, you want the reason someone comments about it to be that they think it's outstanding, not because it tastes like car keys and bad shrimp.

CHRISTMAS

If you're invited to spend Christmas with a family that isn't your own, do not feel awkward; if your host didn't want you there, they wouldn't have invited you. Stop acting like a sad sack and have fun. Buy a little gift for everyone who will be there on Christmas, though don't tell your host you're planning on doing so before you arrive. Otherwise, people will feel obligated to get you something . . . and then you *will* feel awkward. Your gifts don't have to be expensive; think paperback books, good phone chargers, cool socks, wine glasses—you'd be amazed what you can get for twenty bucks if you don't wait till the last minute to shop. If you do receive a gift, don't open it and just say thanks; offer at least one nice thing to say about it even if it's something you'll never use. C'mon, it's Christmas! Be jolly! Jump in to any family traditions or games, because being a house-guest Scrooge is not allowed. Doing something wacky like giving everyone Santa hats with their names on them might seem corny, but it's a fun way to show they haven't invited the Grinch. Besides, all things corny are allowed at Christmas. Get up a little later than your hosts on Christmas morning; that way they'll have some time to exchange gifts with family and you won't have to ooh and ahh during their unwrapping frenzy. Oh, and definitely watch *Elf* before you go; your ability to quote lines from *Elf* will secure your place in the pantheon of all-time great holiday houseguests.

NEW YEAR'S EVE

There are generally two kinds of New Year's houseguest experiences. In one, you're invited to stay with friends, have a quiet dinner, and enjoy some champagne and conversation, and everyone is asleep before midnight. That is the holy grail of New Year's Eves, and if that scenario presents itself, grab it, hug it, and never let it go.

However, if you're a houseguest at New Year's, there's good chance your host will be having a New Year's Eve party, an event that has caused many the severe hangover and served as the inspiration for countless horrible off-Broadway plays. New Year's Eve is amateur night in terms of partying. It's the night that people who rarely drink decide to let loose and whoop it up. Glitter dresses with slits and tuxedo T-shirts come from the back of closets and run wild through the streets. So, as a houseguest, you will have a much better time if you sit back and observe the lunacy around you versus jumping in. Your host will appreciate it if you try to keep things from going off the rails, calling people Ubers, helping find a lost coat (there's always a lost coat), and encouraging the four people together in the bathroom to hurry up. You can still have fun, but don't overdo it. The next-day party rehash is always the best part anyway, and your ability to remember who it was drinking champagne out of an UGG boot will make you the MVP houseguest.

WEDDING WEEKEND

If you're a houseguest during a wedding weekend, your goal is to stay as far away from the wedding insanity as possible. Weddings can cause even the most levelheaded people to become totally unhinged. Though you may not be directly involved with the wedding, your host could be, which means a houseguest (you) may not be their top priority. They're preoccupied with a ring bearer who refuses to wear shoes or finding someone to unclog a chocolate fountain, so cut them a break and be understanding if your accommodations aren't exactly perfect. If you run out of toilet paper, go buy some yourself; if you can't find an extension cord, learn to live with it. You should also ask whether they need help with anything. During a wedding weekend, there are always countless little tasks, so they might appreciate you letting them know you're available if needed. Maybe you can convince that barefoot ring bearer to get with the program.

SORRY, MARTHA

—*Steven Carter-Bailey,* Great British Bake Off *finalist, baker, and podcast host, London*

I know ten ways to fold a napkin, two foolproof methods to rescue dying gravy, and how to turn dried corns husks into a fabulous wreath. This is all due to one woman: Martha Stewart. I've followed Martha's advice on everything from what variety of Christmas tree smells the best (Fraser fir) to how to get red wine stains out of a tablecloth (vinegar, salt, and boiling water). So when my cousin from San Francisco, Fiona, came to stay with me in England over her Thanksgiving break, I naturally turned to Martha to learn how to create an authentic American Thanksgiving.

As a Brit, I knew very little about Thanksgiving. I was aware it involved food, a parade, and yelling at the television while watching football; I would need Martha's guidance for the rest. After looking through countless articles, websites, and books devoted to the holiday, I discovered that a lot goes into creating a true Thanksgiving experience. Of course, the actual holiday is important, but the days leading up to the big day help set the tone, and that tone required a lot of prep work. My cousin is very easy going and would have been fine just eating KFC and watching *Derry Girls* on Thanksgiving, but I tend to get carried away, trying to make everything perfect. (You're dealing with someone who once remade three hundred fondant feathers on a flamingo cake because their shade of pink was a bit too orange.) If Fiona was going to be my houseguest, I wanted to make sure she was hit over the head with Thanksgiving from the moment she arrived.

In the course of my Thanksgiving research, I encountered many terms I was not familiar with. These included "cornucopia" (a horn-shaped object filled with fruit that nobody will ever eat and eventually goes bad), "Black Friday" (an event that happens right after Thanksgiving where Americans beat each other up over flat-screen TVs), and a concoction called "Sweet Potato Marshmallow Casserole." Martha even had a recipe for SPMC (the Sarah Jessica Parker of side dishes), though she elevated it, as always, with fresh, unexpected ingredients like coconut and lime zest.

I also discovered there was an American obsession with something called "pumpkin spice." It was everywhere and in everything, from muffins to Pringles to dog shampoo. If pumpkin spice was an important part of Thanksgiving, I could not deprive my cousin. Thus, I found pumpkin spice potpourri online and put it in the guest bathroom. Fiona could now brush her teeth surrounded by the aroma of what smelled to me like a gingerbread man after a workout.

If I wanted to be a great host and really blow out Thanksgiving, I knew I would need more than a bowl of potpourri, so back to Martha I went for decorating tips. I learned the key to capturing the Thanksgiving spirit is to keep things homespun and rooted in nature. You should avoid store-bought gimmicky decorations—no inflatable turkeys or glitter-covered pumpkins for me. I couldn't fathom why anyone would buy plastic leaves and fiberglass branches when there's a world of *real* ones right outside their door. With that in mind, I set out to transform my flat into a Pilgrim paradise. Martha had so many suggestions it made my head swim. Some were fabulous but outside my time and budget parameters (who wouldn't love a giant marzipan *Mayflower*!), but most were inexpensive and so easy to execute I probably wouldn't even need my trusty glue gun. Side note: invest in a glue gun; it will change your life.

One word kept coming up over and over in Martha's decor suggestions and elsewhere, and that word was "gourd." I'd never given much thought to gourds before, but apparently everyone in serious crafting circles was gaga for gourds. You could delight your guests with gourd masks, gourd vases, gourd dolls, gourd chandeliers, even a gourd xylophone. It was time I jumped on the gourd bandwagon, so I decided to make gourd votive candles. You simply cut off the top, scoop out the gross guck, then pop in a tea candle, and done! They were so fun to make I couldn't stop, so soon my flat was covered in glowing gourds of every shape, size, and hue. I also bought pumpkins of many varieties and colors (white pumpkins, who knew?) and arranged them in tableaus around the house. I gathered beautiful autumn leaves from the park and festooned them together creating a table runner and made leaf garlands that adorned the archways and mantel (THAT'S why you own a glue gun!). I thought my place looked rather magical and hoped Fiona would too. Martha would be proud.

Fiona arrived at my house a day later than planned. She was visiting about a year into the pandemic, so the restrictions in place affected her travel. The rules were changing daily, so we tried to have fun without freaking out over the latest testing and isolation requirements. "What if something happened and I couldn't leave for a year?" asked Fiona. Other hosts might dread the thought of having a houseguest for a long period of time, but I was thrilled at the prospect. I had so many of Martha's ideas yet to try!

One of these ideas was a kicky little Thanksgiving project of Martha's involving hats. Martha had suggested making paper pilgrim hats for the kids' table, but since I was kid-free, I thought they could be fun for the adults. (A tad odd, yes, but we were in the middle of a pandemic, and we'd finished the Escher staircase jigsaw.) Fiona was game, so I got the materials we needed and set about constructing hats for guests to wear at dinner. There were two styles of hats, one for a man Pilgrim and the other for a female Pilgrim. Since the instructions supplied were for child-sized hats, I had to make some adjustments. I think this is where things took a wrong turn. The man's hat was supposed to look like one of those tall black hats with a square gold buckle you see distinguished guys in Dutch masters' paintings wearing. There was nothing distinguished about the thing I constructed; it resembled Pharrell Williams's giant fedora combined with the Arby's logo. The women's hats were more bonnets than hats and looked a thousand percent *Handmaid's Tale*. Fiona and I decided to abandon the idea of hats, though I was somewhat looking forward to Of-Steven jokes.

Since the foray into the millenary world was a bust, I thought it wise to move on to the primary focus of the holiday: food. I had created a spreadsheet to keep track of recipes, shopping lists, utensils needed, cooking times, and serving bowl size required. I was a well-oiled Cuisinart zooming along cooking up a variety of dishes on Martha's Thanksgiving greatest-hits list. Mashed potatoes with sour cream, maple-glazed carrots, cauliflower gratin with chestnuts, cinnamon butternut squash, and two types of dressing (sausage and herb and oyster), and for dessert three pies: apple, lemon chiffon, and the requisite pumpkin. Casseroles seemed to feature prominently in the American Thanksgiving menu. In addition to the aforementioned sweet potato/marshmallow variety, I also made a green bean casserole that called for such exotic ingredients as a can of cream of mushroom soup and crispy fried onions. I started to think that in America the word "casserole" was defined as any hot dish you could slop together with what's left in your cupboard.

With all the sides under control, I moved on to tackling the main event, the turkey. I had never cooked one before, and there were many schools of thought on how to do it properly. You could do everything from deep-frying it, which would result in me singeing off my eyebrows, to splaying it, which I felt stripped the bird of its dignity. I decided to go with Martha's Perfect Turkey 101 recipe, as it seemed the simplest and most traditional. I would pop the turkey in the oven on Thanksgiving morning, and then all the heavy lifting was done. I was really looking forward to relaxing and hanging out with Fiona. I might even revisit the hats.

Thanksgiving morning was going as planned. Fiona slept in, and I made her a pumpkin-spiced latte. She and I then made place cards for the table, writing guest names on leaves that we placed on each dinner plate. Guests would arrive midday, and then we'd eat around 3:00. It was all coming together.

After we got dressed and ready for our feast, Fiona and I began scattering more leaves around the table. It was then that she got an alert on her phone. Her flight scheduled for tomorrow had been canceled, and if she wanted to get back to San Francisco this week, she would have to leave Thanksgiving evening due to limited flights during the pandemic. Fiona felt horrible about the change of plans, and I assured her it was no problem, as I saw my vision of the picture-perfect Thanksgiving rapidly fading.

As Fiona ran to pack, guests started arriving, and I explained the situation. When I checked on the progress of the turkey, it was nowhere near being cooked. It was a light beige color with white spots, as if it had a very bad spray tan. I was determined to get the turkey Instagram ready, so I cranked up the temperature in the oven.

Once Fiona was packed, I seated everyone at the table. I received rave reviews for my table design; guests loved the place cards, leaf table runners, and gourd votives. Martha was doing me proud. I served the side dishes, which people enjoyed, but the meal seemed quite naked without the bird on the table.

As I checked the time, I knew it was now or never to present the turkey. I took the bird from the oven, and it now had a pale brown glow. I was confident that with the right camera filter, I could capture a real Norman Rockwell Thanksgiving moment, with the guests all smiling as I placed the turkey on the table.

I transferred the turkey to the giant platter I bought on eBay and carried it in the dining room. Guests made the "ooh" and "ahh" sounds I was hoping for as I brought the bird in for a landing in the center of the table. As I started to put it down, the edge of the platter bumped into a gourd votive, knocking a lit tea candle onto the dried leaf table runner. I suddenly realized why people bought fake fireproof leaves when the table runner caught fire and exploded in flames that shot down the length of the table. I was amazed how quickly it spread. It was as if I was attempting some Las Vegas–type stunt where I carried a turkey through a wall of flames. Guests threw water on the flames and hit the burning leaves with their napkins. The fire was soon out, leaving charred leaves, a scorched tablecloth, and wet everything else in its wake. Apparently, dried leaves and branches mixed with rubber cement glue is right up on top of the combustible pyramid. Why didn't I just toss in some turpentine-soaked rags to really get things going?

When I eventually cut into the bird, it was pretty much raw throughout, so in addition to setting my guests ablaze, I could also offer them food poisoning. With the smell of a bonfire in the air, guests seemed to lose their appetite anyway, and it was time for Fiona to head to the airport. I gave her some pie to eat on the plane, though considering how the day was going, TSA agents would probably confiscate it.

I went back to reread Martha's advice on burning candles, and she was very clear about keeping them away from anything that could easily ignite; I guess I missed that part during my gourd frenzy. I am still a devoted fan and will forever follow her advice on all things food and decorating. It wasn't her fault I almost burned my building down.

I still love being a host and having houseguests. I just wish I had given Fiona a better Thanksgiving. But one little house fire won't stop me. I try to remember there's always another houseguest and another holiday. Besides, I can't wait to make Martha's Halloween Frankenstein out of empty soup cans and kale.

Length of Stay and Obligation to Host

CHAPTER 13

SUNNY AND SHARING

The Houseguest and the Group Share

The house share is a situation where a small group of people stay together and equally share the cost of lodgings and other expenses and discover what each other look like in their underwear. House shares are quite popular in areas near beaches with overpriced produce stands and establishments that sell countless varieties of fudge. MTV's *Jersey Shore* popularized the house share concept, though not all house share experiences need be quite as "primal" as those of Snooki and her duck à la root beer–hued friends. It is possible to be a houseguest with others and have a great time; you just need to be prepared for a few houseguest land mines.

EARLY BIRDS ARE SPECIAL

The earlier you arrive at a house share, the better your chances are of securing a good place to sleep. As you'd expect, the best rooms go first, so if you're one of the last guests to arrive, you may discover that where you're sleeping looks suspiciously like a dog bed. Never operate on the belief that one of your friends who arrived earlier will reserve a room for you. Even if they try to claim a space for you, they will be overruled. As soon as you arrive, make sure to quickly mark your territory, and merely saying "I call the blue room" won't cut it. Put your things in the room you want immediately, then open your luggage and toss things around so that it looks lived in. A half-eaten Twix or an open contact lens case on the nightstand will telegraph to others in the pack that this room is taken. Then later on someone can't claim they didn't realize you meant *that* blue room. If you really want a specific room, stand your ground; room bullies abound, so don't cave that easily. You don't want things to get too contentious, but a quick round of "rock paper scissors" should solve things.

Something to consider is that the best rooms aren't always the most obvious. A room with a terrace might seem awesome at first glance, but its proximity to the home's main living area could prove trouble when that 3:00 a.m. beer pong game moves into overtime and you're trying to sleep.

MONEY CHANGES EVERYTHING

The last thing you want to deal with on vacation is people getting weird about money. Some people are very casual about dividing house expenses, while others will be pulling out their calculator every two minutes, announcing the amount everyone owes. Before committing to a house share, make sure everyone involved is on the same page in terms of how costs will be divided. Food and drink are usually the largest expenses, so ask how the group plans to handle meals. Some groups like to split up and do their own thing at mealtime, while others like to all eat together. If you all dine together at a restaurant, you need to decide whether you want to be THAT TABLE who forces your server to juggle a handful of credit cards or have one individual pick up the check one night and another person the next, etc. If you know your fellow houseguests well, this method usually works best. Since you're on vacation, you should expect to spend more money than you normally would, so don't whine about how expensive a restaurant is, as that will bum everyone out. If you feel a restaurant is vastly beyond your budget, simply don't go; however, don't make a big deal out of it. You will not eat a frozen pizza in front of your fellow houseguests and tell them to enjoy their "fancy dinner." No, that will not happen.

The cost of groceries for the house can be more easily divided, so make a list before the designated shopper heads to the store. It's totally fine to request a certain brand of cereal that others can share in (who hates Rice Krispies?), but if you want some pricey brand of anchovies, buy it yourself. Sharing grocery costs is for things like coffee, eggs, and paper towels, not Marlboro Lights. Similarly, buy your own liquor but be prepared for it to disappear rather quickly. Fellow houseguests have few boundaries when it comes to booze, so don't get all huffy when your bottle of Patrón seems to have evaporated overnight. You need to remember that it's a group house and every houseguest's feathers will be ruffled at some point. And, please, do *not* keep your liquor stashed in your room away from the group; if you do, it will be the one thing everyone talks about after the trip. "He told me all the bourbon was gone, but he hid it in his golf bag!"

SLOBS VERSUS NEAT FREAKS

Mayonnaise smeared on a countertop can cause some people to retch, while others become enraged at the sound of a vacuum cleaner. When you're a group houseguest, you'll quickly see on what end of the cleanliness spectrum you and fellow houseguests fall. Some people are just gross, and they don't realize (or care) about cleanliness or germs or mess. The notion of changing the sheets never crosses their mind, milk is never put back in the refrigerator, and their dirty dishes stay dirty until one of their fellow houseguests washes them. You can try to use humor to get them to clean up after themselves, saying things like "Whoever left the milk out on the counter, it's rapidly turning into cottage cheese, so please put it back in the refrigerator," but such brilliant comedy will be lost on them. Most of the time it's easier to just sigh and do what you need done yourself. Another approach that can be oddly effective is to loudly bark out whatever slovenly behavior you observe as if it's a news bulletin. "Wet towel on floor! Wet towel on floor!" Yes, you'll sound like a malfunctioning robot, but it's a way to communicate there's an issue without assigning any blame.

The obsessively neat are usually a godsend in a group houseguest situation. They may even bring their own Windex and Swiffers, as they worry their preferred brand of cleaning products won't be available where they're going. (This stems from a Scrubbing Bubbles shortage they once experienced in Peru.) The only real problem you might encounter with the neat freak is that they are prone to snatching your glass or plate away while you're still using it. Turn for even a moment and you'll be asking, "Did anybody see my coffee?" This behavior can be remedied either by writing your name on a coffee mug in an aggressive scrawl or catching them in the act. The neat freak will claim they weren't aware you were using it, but the cold stare you give them will communicate that you both know the truth.

CHAPTER 14

WHO WAS THAT MASKED GUEST?

The Houseguest during the Pandemic

Not that it could ever, ever, ever happen, but what if a global pandemic started when a weird virus escaped from a lab or when a pig ate a sick bat or—wait, *what?* Gosh, that's sure going to take this chapter in a different direction.

A pandemic is not fun and affects people in crazy, unexpected ways. Prior to the arrival of Covid, few people took pride in their extensive hand sanitizer knowledge or had strong opinions on their favorite celebrity epidemiologist. The pandemic has also created whole new varieties of houseguests.

LET'S APOCALYPSE TOGETHER

During a pandemic, especially during lockdown, many singles realize that watching every episode of *Normal People* alone isn't that fun and opt to find someone to share isolation with. Choosing this person requires a great deal of thought, as you want someone you can trust as well as someone who won't drive you completely insane after three days. Prior to having someone as a long-term houseguest, you may not be aware of some of their habits and idiosyncrasies that making living with them pure hell. Under normal circumstances, the fact that this person talks to the television ("Are you crazy? Do **not** go in that attic!") wouldn't bother you that much. However, once you're cohabitating, you are convinced that any court of law would acquit you for whatever you were forced to do to make your guest stop doing that. It's best to be direct when inviting someone into an isolation houseguest arrangement. Ask things like: are they prone to screaming in the middle of the night, do they have any food preferences that will stink up your refrigerator, and do they watch *Wheel of Fortune?* Facts such as these make it perfectly permissible to tell someone, "I'm afraid this isn't going to work out."

During a pandemic, individuals might also choose to have a living arrangement with someone who is more than platonic. It's somewhat like a business deal, where both parties realize that casual Tinder-ing is probably not the smartest thing to do with a highly contagious virus floating around. So a friends-with-benefits arrangement is coordinated. If both parties are on the same page in terms of expectations in this situation, it can work out great. Though if after a couple weeks the houseguest starts talking about how they want to remodel the kitchen, this would be considered a red flag.

LET THE RIGHT ONE IN

Due to no fault of their own, during a pandemic some people are forced to look for a new place to stay for a variety of reasons. When this *28 Days Later*–type situation occurs, the houseguest needs to follow all rules set down by the host, even if they don't agree with them. If a host wants you to wear a mask, you wear a mask; if they want you to spray disinfectant whenever you use the bathroom, you spray disinfectant; if they want you to wrap your feet in plastic bags and do a little Irish jig before you come in the house, you do it. It doesn't matter what your host asks you to do; you just do it without discussion or debate. You should be beyond appreciative that someone is actually giving you a place to stay when others are moving furniture in front of their doors screaming, "Go away! I've got bear spray, and I'll use it!"

A pandemic is a very stressful time, so a host may be more on edge than usual. If you're a houseguest and the host snaps at you for buttering your toast too loudly, don't take it personally; it's not your buttering technique but the anxiety from watching the world crumble that's making your host a little testy.

POD PEOPLE

Humans are social animals, much like chimpanzees but with a lot less preening and eating fleas off each other. However, during lockdown you're forced to talk to the same people day after day and have every possible conversation there is to have, multiple times. ("Yes, you told me about the time you met Jimmy Fallon.") So it's understandable that after a long time in isolation, you'd want to safely expand your social circle. This is accomplished by bringing in houseguests to your living situation and creating a "quarantine bubble." This bubble is made up of people you trust who also see the benefit of social interaction and who don't have horrible taste in movies and TV shows.

Isolation isn't healthy for anyone, and neither is anxiety, so make sure that your pod of pandemic people get along. In any good, predictable horror movie, there's always the jerk of the group who does something stupid and selfish that lets the monster in. Soon everybody is a goner, except for the actor with the highest box office appeal. This can happen to your quarantine pod too. If someone doesn't follow the agreed-upon rules of the group, they put everyone at risk, and that swab up your nose may soon be telling you things you don't want to hear.

A LITTLE BIT NAZI AND A LITTLE BIT ROCK 'N' ROLL

—Tom Coleman

I had never been to Arizona. The only thing I really knew about it was that it's always a zillion degrees and people there wear a lot of turquoise jewelry. So when my old work friend Karl invited me for the weekend, I accepted, as I was already in Los Angeles on business and Phoenix was a quick, cheap flight. It was at the tail end of the pandemic, and it felt good to be traveling again. Plus, it was hot and sticky back in New York City, and Karl had a pool.

I had not seen Karl in "real life" in about twelve years. I would soon realize that twelve years is a rather long time. It's the length of primary and secondary school combined and the average life of a dachshund. I would learn that people can change a lot in twelve years and that just because you like someone's tomato plant photos on Instagram doesn't mean you have any remote connection to them after ten-plus years.

My first hint that Karl may have changed a tiny bit from the last time I saw him was when he picked me up at the airport on Friday. This was soon after Covid vaccines were approved, and Karl was wearing a hat that read "Not Vaxxed, Not Sheep." I wasn't sure what that meant, but he soon informed me as he launched into a diatribe about vaccinations, Bill Gates, and how nobody was going to tell him what to put into his body. I looked out the window and sighed as he honked and zoomed wildly through traffic.

The fact that I was fully vaccinated put my mind somewhat at ease, but it was Karl's somewhat unhinged behavior that worried me. The Karl I remembered was intense but a lot of fun. He was in a metal band that did covers of Iron Maiden *and* the Carpenters, and I once watched him eat an entire tube of toothpaste on a dare. This new Karl was angry at the world, especially with his ex-wife and the IRS—or maybe it was the IRA; at one point there was a rant about Lucky Charms changing the ratio of moons to clovers, so they may have been responsible.

Karl lived in a nice ranch house in a golf course community. The house was decorated in nonthreatening early Pottery Barn, and nothing really stood out except for a large glass display cabinet. The cabinet took up an entire wall of the dining room and was filled with white porcelain figurines. OK, a little odd, but everybody needs a hobby. They looked similar to those Lladró statues you see in duty-free shops, but in all white. There were about fifty in a wide variety of twee subjects including cows, fauns, maidens carrying baskets, children on swings, and oddly a lot of German shepherds. I made a mental note to ask Karl about his collection, as it seemed like a safe topic of conversation.

Things were going fairly smoothly. On Saturday, I sat by the pool and read while Karl ran errands. He was hosting a barbecue with a few friends that evening, and since I was leaving early Sunday, I figured I could easily skate through a night of small talk and shish kebabs and head home from my time as a houseguest unscathed.

The barbecue guests included a chatty lawyer couple, Brian and Sarah; Curtis, an architect who spoke very deliberately and didn't use contractions; and his wife, Marina, an artist who was apparently an authority on everything. "In Turkey, shish kebab would never be served with meat and vegetable on the same skewer. I mean NEVER."

Conversation with the guests centered around travel, real estate, and the occasional jab at the fact that I lived New York City. Yes, please go ahead and make fun of seven-dollar lattes and rats as big as watermelons if it means we stay away from politics, global warming, or other incendiary topics.

As we ate our non-Turkey-approved shish kebabs on Karl's deck, everyone starting making little jokes about what was going to happen after dinner. "Karl, do you think your friend is prepared for this?" said chatty lawyer husband. "This is going to be fun to watch!" said wife Sarah. "Well, we'll soon find out," chuckled Karl. Of course, like anyone else, my mind immediately jumped to devil worship. That's why I was invited! They needed an out-of-state, hard-to-trace human sacrifice, or at the very least, they were going to make me kill a goat. "Should we use mine?" said contraction-free Curtis. "It is in the car." Karl nodded, and Curtis headed toward the driveway. I looked around the deck for something to use to defend myself against the ancient dagger or paralyzing dart that Curtis went to retrieve from his Subaru.

Everyone started to clear the long wooden dinner table that would undoubtedly serve as the sacrificial altar. Curtis returned with a canvas bag, the kind you get when you make a donation to PBS and don't want the Andrea Bocelli DVD, and placed it in the center of the table. Curtis nodded toward Karl as if to say "It is time." Karl put his hand in the bag and pulled out a small square box, and it was then I learned my fate and understood the reason why everyone was really there that night. We were going to play Yahtzee.

When I played Yahtzee as a kid, it was usually on rainy days when you couldn't find all the pieces to Monopoly. It was a harmless little dice game that was a great afternoon time filler. This Yahtzee was something altogether different. Karl and his friends were VERY serious about their Yahtzee. They entered tournaments, played online with people around the world, and wagered big money. As we began playing, I had forgotten a few of the rules and could sense my questions did not sit well with the group, especially Curtis. His heavy sighs and leg bouncing seemed to suggest that playing with an amateur was working his last nerve. Karl also seemed to be losing patience with my clumsy Yahtzee play, as signaled by his clenched teeth and "C'mon, c'mon" whenever it was my turn. "Did you know Yahtzee was invented by a Canadian couple who used to play it on their yacht?" offered Marina in an attempt to lighten the mood or secure her place as the ultimate Yahtzee insider.

We were halfway through the game, and it was my turn again. In an attempt to not dawdle and move the game along, I accidentally gave an overly enthusiastic shake of the cup holding the dice, causing two of them to fly off the table and across the deck. With that, Curtis pushed himself away from the table and stood and yelled (without contractions), "That is it; I am done. He is BETRAYING the game!" *Betraying the game?* I thought. This wasn't Fischer versus Spassky; it was Yahtzee! Marina tried to calm Curtis down by saying, "Honey, he doesn't know any better," as if I were a dimwitted Labrador. I thought Karl would come to my defense, because I was his houseguest after all, but instead he apologized to the others saying, "I should have known better; he doesn't understand." Understand what? You throw dice on a table and count.

The evening broke up soon after. Guests said their goodbyes, and Karl continued apologizing as I pretended to clean the kitchen. They all gave me halfhearted waves as they walked out the door, and I knew the theme of their discussions on the way home would be "Well, that's New York City for you."

Karl seemed kind of angry when he came into the kitchen. I considered whether to discuss the "incident" or pretend nothing had happened. Since I was leaving in the morning and hate all nervous, weird conversations, I went with the latter. "Do the kebab skewers go in the dishwasher?" I asked. Karl gave a quick nod as he grabbed a bottle of water from the refrigerator and left the room without looking at me. He had gone all seventh-grade girl and wasn't speaking to me, and I was totally fine with that. I knew I had done nothing wrong aside from not being a Yahtzee-obsessed freak. Plus, in a matter of hours I would be sitting on a plane headed home.

I got up early the next morning to pack, and I could hear Karl puttering in the kitchen. When I went in to get coffee, his mood seemed to have improved as he said "Good morning" and handed me a mug as he turned down the blaring Def Leppard without me having to ask. Apparently, I would no longer have to wear a scarlet Y on my chest to atone for my Yahtzee sins. I decided to move on from the night before as I didn't want to poke the unstable bear. Plus, I wanted a ride to the airport.

I needed an innocuous topic to discuss till I was ready to leave for my flight. I decided this would be a good time to ask Karl about his cabinet full of porcelain figurines. There couldn't be anything controversial about statues of fauns and farmers, right? He seemed eager to talk about the figures, and his face lit up when I asked about them. "Oh, you noticed them. Well, I'm somewhat of a collector," he said. We walked from the kitchen to the cabinet in the dining room, where the figures were. "This one is very valuable," he said, opening the cabinet and taking out an antlered stag to show me. "You rarely see Allach porcelain of this quality, and you never see so much in one collection," Karl said, proudly gesturing to his array of animals and peasants. "Allach porcelain? I've never heard of that," I said, somewhat interested while trying to keep the conversation light and breezy. "German, mid-twentieth century. Highly skilled craftsmen made these," he said. "You are a fount of knowledge, Karl," I said, attempting to puff up my host and secure that ride to the airport. Karl smiled as he closed the cabinet, and I went back to the guest room to finish packing.

As I packed, I kept thinking about what Karl had said about the porcelain being German and from the middle part of the twentieth century and got a creepy feeling. I went to my phone and looked up Allach porcelain. The creepy feeling quickly turned into room spinning when I saw the words "Allach porcelain," "Third Reich," and "Himmler." I was suddenly Mia Farrow in *Rosemary's Baby*, realizing my neighbors weren't just a wacky old couple. "Allach porcelain was created by artisans imprisoned in Dachau concentration camp during World War Two, under the direct supervision of the infamous SS, and was prized by its brutal and murderous leader, Heinrich Himmler." I sat down on the bed to compose myself, realizing there was basically a Nazi shrine down the hall. Maybe Karl wasn't aware of the porcelain's horrific past, I thought. But if I could find out about the porcelain in a five-second Google search, he had to know. Other people collect baseball cards or snow globes; I was staying with someone who thought it was fun to fill his house with tchotchkes made by Hitler's death squad.

Despite hating confrontation, I knew it would haunt me if I didn't say something to Karl about his "collection." I found him in the front hall winding a cuckoo clock. "Ready to go?" Karl asked. "Traffic to the airport shouldn't be that bad; all the snowflakes are still afraid to fly," he added. "Karl, um, I was just doing a little research on your porcelain. Did you know it was made by prisoners of the SS . . . as in Hitler's SS?" I asked. "Oh yeah, the SS had a great appreciation for the arts," he said as he continued winding. "Yeah, they also had an appreciation for torture and murder. Karl, collecting Nazi stuff is NOT cool!" I said, trying not to add "you lunatic." Karl sighed. "It's *history*; the porcelain is part of *history*," he said shaking his head. "Yeah, it was the darkest time in history, and they forced people in concentration camps to make all your weird little birds and sheep," I said, knowing I would soon lose my shit. Karl looked at me incredulously and said, "They **liked** making the porcelain; it gave them something to do!" An actual human being was trying to tell me that Holocaust prisoners viewed forced labor as a "fun hobby" that broke up the monotony. I tried to think of an eloquent response to this, but all I came up with was "You are fucking nuts."

I took an Uber to the airport and have stopped eating shish kebab, and if I ever hear the sound of rattling dice, I'm worse than a dog on the Fourth of July.

CHAPTER 15

WELL, THAT WAS DIFFERENT

The Houseguest in Unusual Places

Occasionally, you're invited to be a houseguest somewhere that's a little out of the ordinary. When this happens, you're initially elated at the prospect of sleeping in a teepee or spending the weekend on an ice floe . . . and then it dawns on you that you'll be sleeping in a teepee or spending a weekend on an ice floe for an EN-tire weekend. Staying someplace unusual usually goes one of two ways: either it's a memorable life event you'll always treasure or it causes night sweats and spontaneous muttering of "Sweet Jesus, what was I thinking?"

THEMED EVENTS

When you arrive, your host gives you a top hat, a fake mustache, and a velvet opera cape. You must wear these items throughout your stay, as you assume the role of Lord Nigel Eaton-Bacon, who may be the killer of Lady Cecily Von Snooty, the reclusive cough syrup heiress.

If the previous paragraph made you groan or wince even a tiny bit, take that as a sign you're not cut out for a Murder Mystery Weekend, *Game of Thrones*-athon, LEGO and Lace experience, or any other themed event. Don't feel bad about it; some people have an aversion to themed events so ingrained in their DNA it's absolutely impossible for them to enjoy themselves. Even if you genuinely want to go, your body will involuntarily react with heavy sighs, head shaking, and incredulous gasps. When you accept an invitation to a themed event, there can be no sniping or eye-rolling; you must fully embrace the concept and enthusiastically join in, as otherwise there's no point in going. Your host has no doubt gone to a lot of effort to organize this event, so you will not be raining or even light drizzling on their parade. Either put on the opera cape and fully commit or stay home.

THE WHITE HOUSE

Let's say you help land a jetliner in a cornfield after the pilot eats a bad turkey wrap or you assist a Secret Service agent in thwarting a presidential dognapping. Next thing you know, you're getting a call about a little slumber party at 1600 Pennsylvania Avenue. Politics goes out the window, and it doesn't matter whether the current resident is red, blue, or chartreuse if you somehow snag an invitation to stay at the White House. Nobody should pass up the opportunity to sleep in the same bed as such great Americans as Abraham Lincoln, Franklin Delano Roosevelt, and Barbra Streisand.

The primary reason to stay at the White House is, of course, bragging rights. Yes, we know you're passionate about history and would be honoured (with a *u*) to spend time in a place with such an illustrious past. Though when your neighbor Larry won't stop babbling about the suite he had in Maui, with a *free* minibar, you'll experience unbounded glee when you shut him down by offering him M&M's embossed with the presidential seal.

Concrete proof that you were a houseguest at the White House is important. Taking things home that confirm your stay is allowed, within reason. You can't cut up the carpet in the Oval Office, but if an item in your room is adorned with that prized presidential seal and it can fit in your carry-on, it's fair game. Pens, stationery, soap, playing cards—if it truly is the people's house, this people is taking home a hair dryer.

During your stay, try to see as much of the White House as possible and photograph whatever you can without getting tackled by security. Everybody has seen the Oval Office, so attempt to gain access to places that prove you stayed there and weren't on some guided tour you bought at your kid's school fundraiser. The White House bowling alley, the secret indoor pool, and that pantry where Bill Clinton liked to hold, um, "meetings" should be on your list.

HAUNTED HOUSE

When you're a houseguest, usually the only time things go bump in the night is when you trip over your luggage looking for the light switch. However, if while settling into your room your host casually mentions, "Oh, if you see a translucent little girl in a Victorian dress standing at the foot of your bed, that's just Arabella, our ghost," you should know how to react. You don't want to instantly go into paranormal naysayer mode and start spewing facts you learned on some Discovery Channel show. Since your host brought it up, they obviously want to talk about their see-through housemate, so seem interested. Ask whether their ghost is friendly, in the tradition of Casper, or whether it is more of the cranky variety that wants to inhabit your body and claim your soul. It doesn't matter whether you're a believer; if your host thinks their house is haunted, there is zero harm in playing along. The level to which you play along is up to you. You can go full *Poltergeist* and tell tales at breakfast of levitating beds and apparitions in the mirror or simply agree that you also "feel a presence." This presence can come in handy, too, especially if you accidentally break something during your stay. "That Arabella sure is a prankster! I mean, how else could that lamp have fallen off the dresser?"

DOOMSDAY BUNKER

There was a time when doomsday bunkers were concrete underground boxes or hollowed-out school buses wrapped in tinfoil, owned by survivalists who kept looking at the window waiting for the Rapture. Well, doomsday bunkers aren't just for crazy people anymore! Bunkers now come with all the comforts of home and are equipped with everything from wine cellars to hot tubs, allowing owners to relax in subterranean luxury while the rest of humanity withers and dies up above.

Your houseguest experience at a doomsday bunker will vary, depending on the level of doom you find yourself in. If your host built the bunker as more of a novelty to show off to guests during doom-free times, then your main concern is whether you really want to spend an extended period of time underground with this person. Someone who builds a doomsday bunker as a way to say "Look at me, look at me, I've got so much disposable income, I can build a kooky underground house!" is likely to get on your nerves. Keep in mind that when you're a thousand feet beneath the earth, you can't exactly run out for coffee to take a breather.

If your bunker invitation comes during a time that's doom-heavy, you can't be picky if your choices are retreat to the bunker or take on a zombie invasion with a staple gun. Once you're in the bunker, your primary concern is doing all you can to maintain harmony within the group. You've seen *Survivor*; it's always the prickly ones who get voted out first. Don't cause any trouble; otherwise, you may be forced to leave the bunker, or if you're really annoying, they'll eat you.

CHAPTER 16

DO NOT FLUSH THE FOLLOWING

Houseguest Rules

When you're a houseguest, you're never sure about house rules. Some hosts have zero rules, and their relaxed attitude suggests that as long as you don't burn the place down, they're pretty much fine with whatever you do. Other hosts are more rigid; you pick up on this when they hand you a binder upon arrival that covers what **is** and **is not** allowed in regard to every aspect of your stay (showers shall not exceed six minutes and no red or blush wine near the white sofa). You should assume things such as no smoking indoors and always taking off your shoes when you come inside, but if you're not sure about other things, ask. It's better to find out before you innocently break a house rule and are corrected by your host—or, worse, shamed by an eight-year-old who informs you, "Mommy doesn't want you using those glasses." So ask, ask away. While your host's rules may not be printed up and posted in your room, there are some areas where using a little common sense will help you avoid some uncomfortable moments during your stay.

FOOD

Even if your host tells you to help yourself to whatever you want, you should definitely buy some groceries during your visit and pick up a couple things that you know your host likes. A few muffins and some fresh-squeezed orange juice can do wonders for your houseguest standing. If you cook, try to do so when your host isn't in the kitchen to keep from getting in their way. Don't make anything that stinks up the whole house or cook any elaborate meals. No soufflés or anything that requires thirteen bowls and every utensil in the drawer—keep it basic and clean up when finished. Don't leave dirty dishes in the sink; wash them by hand or put them in the dishwasher. People are very particular about their dishwashers, and how they load them is a precise science. There's a 99.9 percent chance you won't load it to your host's satisfaction, so this is a good time to ask for help.

Eating in your room should be limited to snacks. Spilling gazpacho all over the duvet would not be appreciated. If you bring any mugs or bowls to your room, make sure you return them to the kitchen before science projects start growing in the bottom.

HOUSEKEEPING

Make your bed. There's something crime scene-y about an unmade bed; you expect to see yellow tape across the door and those little cards with numbers on them scattered around the room. The bed doesn't need to be perfect, but at least pull up the bedding and stack the pillows so it isn't a disheveled mess. Your host will be happy when they poke their head in your room, and somewhere your mother will smile and not know why.

Keep all your belongings and clothes in your room and hang things up or fold them. It takes only a couple minutes to maintain some degree of order. Before you leave, clean up your space and bring any trash to the garbage. Always do one final sweep of the room to make sure you aren't leaving anything behind. Look under the bed, in the closet, and behind chairs and check wall outlets for any chargers. This way, in about a month, you won't receive a mystery package from your host that contains a T-shirt, three socks, and an earbud case.

CONSIDERATION

While your host isn't likely to give you a curfew, you should make an effort to come home at a reasonable hour. Even if you think you're being "really quiet," as you stumble in at the same time the garbage men are arriving, you're not, and you may wake the entire house. This will inevitably lead to a nervous conversation where you feel obligated to provide details as to why you got home so late. To avoid all this, adhere to the adage that nothing good happens after 2:00 a.m. Yes, many *fun* things can happen after 2:00 a.m. but nothing *good*; there's a difference, so head home and reward yourself with a big breakfast the next morning. Order two cinnamon rolls, because you deserve it.

You could be guilty of some behaviors that seem perfectly harmless to you but will secretly drive your host crazy. If you're a cologne or perfume wearer, you should keep the spritzing to a minimum. It doesn't matter whether it's expensive and endorsed by Charlize Theron; your idea of wearing *a little* can be overwhelming to others. Some hosts are allergic, some hosts hate cologne, and some hosts just hate *your* cologne. Regardless, when you're a houseguest, dial down your fragrance wearing or turn it off completely. Similarly, if you're a spray tanner, either bring your own sheets or halt all bronzing during your stay. Leaving an orange-brownish residue all over your host's nice white sheets is something often referred to as super gross.

A RECIPE FOR GETTING ASKED BACK

Every houseguest must have at least ONE foolproof recipe in their repertoire. It should be something easy to make that's a guaranteed crowd pleaser and won't take over your host's kitchen with a million dirty bowls and appliances. By contributing to a meal, it shows that you're really appreciative of your host's efforts and makes you one of the gang. Plus, you can all talk about how much you love *The Bear* as you chop and dice together and call each other "chef."

The Aren't-I-A-Good-Guest Corn Salad

Serves: 4 to 6 people as a side dish

3 or 4 ears of corn

3 medium ripe tomatoes, chopped

6–8 ounces feta cheese,
   about 1 ½ cup

½ cup chopped fresh mint leaves

3 tablespoons extra-virgin olive oil

Salt and freshly ground
   black pepper

Optional:

1 cup seedless watermelon chunks

Jalapeno, diced

NOTES ON INGREDIENTS

Fresh corn is best. Shuck it first, then rub a little olive oil on the ears. Place them directly on the outdoor grill until they blacken up and char a bit (they should look a little like that corn you hang on your door at Thanksgiving). If they make a popcorn noise, that's fine. Let them cool slightly, then hold the ear vertically and slice the corn kernels off. Don't use a sharp knife, as you'll end screaming "Band-Aid, stat!" Any standard dinner knife should work. If you don't have a grill, slice the corn off the cob and blacken it in a frying pan on the stove over medium heat. You can also cook the corn in the microwave. Shuck the corn, wrap it in a damp towel, and zap it for about 60 seconds. Frozen corn is allowed if fresh is out of season or if you're a lazy person.

Use good tomatoes. If possible, get the fun-colored heirloom variety. They taste better and look cooler in the salad. Plus, people will comment on them, thus firmly establishing you as a salad slayer. Chop the tomatoes, but not too small or the salad will get mushy.

Don't be stingy with the feta. People really like it, and they'll get sad when they poke through their salad and realize it's all gone.

Yes, you DO need the fresh mint and, NO, you can't substitute it with something else (stop looking at the Tic Tacs). Most good-sized super-markets carry it. It's usually in the produce area where they use that mister thingy.

Extra-virgin olive oil. Use the good kind.

Salt and pepper. This is an important ingredient that's easy to forget, so don't. Remember that when people don't "season" their dish on *Top Chef*, they always get sent home and Tom and Padma shake their heads in disgust.

OPTIONAL INGREDIENTS

In spring/summer, add a cup of chopped seedless watermelon. Don't use too much or it makes things watery and gross. You can also add a little diced jalapeno, but don't go crazy with it.

PREPARATION

Step 1   In a medium bowl, combine the corn, tomatoes, feta cheese, and mint. Drizzle with the olive oil and toss to coat.

Step 2   Season to taste with salt and pepper. Serve.

Step 3   You're all done and everyone loves you and your salad! Go take a nap.

WHO ELSE IS COMING?
Dealing with Fellow Houseguests

B efore you accept an invitation as a houseguest, every fiber of your being wants to say, "That sounds great; however, I need to know who else is going to be there, and if I don't like them, there is no way in hell I'm coming." But of course, you can't. You can try to weasel the guest list out of your host, but hosts are clever and fully realize you want this information. They don't want people suddenly remembering they have fake commitments once they hear who else is coming. Hosts will reply to your passive-aggressive inquiries with statements like "It's a fun mix" or "Some people you know; some you don't." Yes, you should just be thankful you got invited, but c'mon—it would be great to have a little advance warning as to whom you are going to be dealing with during your stay. How else will you be able to Google them and spend hours dissecting their Facebook photos?

In the event you don't know who else will be joining you as houseguest, you should be prepared for anyone and know exactly how to handle them.

THE KNOW-IT-ALL

Mention any city, musician, restaurant, disease, breed of dog . . . basically mention *any* topic and they will know more about it than you, your host, or any other houseguest. Correction: they will know more about it than anyone else in the world. The Know-It-All likes to monopolize conversations, and their opinions are usually culled from other people's Twitter and Facebook posts. Don't be surprised if after one of the Know-It-All's authoritative declarations, someone says, "Funny, Chrissy Teigen said the same thing about global warming." Never challenge the Know-It-All, even if you are sure that something they say is incorrect, because it serves no purpose and will just make your host and other guests nervous and weird. Things will become very quiet, and all of a sudden everyone will need to take a nap. If being a Know-It-All is how they get joy out of life, what real harm is it causing, aside from destroying the conversation? If their interminable know-it-all-ness gets too maddening, remove yourself from the conversation by volunteering to do a task, such as walking the dog or going to the store for more lemons. OK, maybe not lemons; the Know-It-All would no doubt go into a lengthy explanation of why the Lisbon variety of lemons is best for cocktails. "Of course, the Lisbon lemon isn't originally from Portugal." ICE, go get more ice.

THE SHOCKER

The goal of the Shocker is to shock fellow houseguests, though the methods they employ are varied. Upon being introduced to a Shocker, they'll quickly test you with something basic to gauge your reaction. Perhaps they'll pepper their conversation with lots of profanity, building to excessive c-word usage. When the potty mouth strategy doesn't work, Shockers quickly move on to sharing intimate details of their sex life. Shocker couples often use this approach, casually relaying information most people would tell only their urologist. Shocker couples will also use public displays of "get a room" to shock.

Shocker houseguests love to be contrarians on most any topic and will blurt personal facts as a means to shock. Since this is their objective, it's fun to appear totally unfazed and actually encourage them to be more shocking. While it may be difficult to maintain your composure when they tell you about the *Kama Sutra* coloring book they're working on with their six-year-old or say they think Charles Manson was an "underrated genius," you can do it. Your host will appreciate you tolerating the Shocker, and you definitely won't be the most offensive houseguest.

THE NEW BEST FRIEND

You have barely put your luggage down when the New Best Friend begins to tell you all about their life and expects you to do the same. During your stay, this houseguest, whom you have never met before, will instantly assume you want to sit next to them at meals and go on errands together, and, yes, you **will** be on their charades team. At first you might be flattered that someone finds you so fascinating, but when they start saying things like "That's so you" after knowing you two hours and offering to let you use their toothbrush when you already *have* a toothbrush, this signals that you may be wandering into *Single White Female* territory. The New Best Friend will agree with anything you say, nodding enthusiastically like a bobblehead, and will love and hate the same things you do. "You like olives too? That's just freaky!"

You might start to feel guilty and consider that maybe you're a jerk. Is it really so bad if someone wants to be your friend? So what if they start talking about a trip you two will take to Iceland and ask for your sweater size because they want to knit you something? You can take solace in knowing that you did the right thing and that there's no possible way you will ever see this person again.

SOMEBODY'S GOT A SECRET

When you're a houseguest with a Secret Keeper, you've basically got all the entertainment you need during your stay. A Secret Keeper is someone you instantly sense is hiding something about who they are, something they've done, or something they plan to do. You can turn this into a fun game by making it your mission to discover exactly what it is they're hiding during your time together. Sometimes it's not that difficult to figure out. The dude who makes frequent trips to the bathroom, sniffs a lot, and talks nonstop for twenty minutes before going to the bathroom again is kind of a no-brainer. However, sometimes it takes a bit more sleuthing. Secret Keepers subliminally want to be found out and will offer clues with statements such as "I think I was away then" (spent time in the Big House), "Sorry, I don't have any cash on me" (bad scratch-off habit), and "My dating situation is complicated" (wildly bisexual).

THE PARTY MONSTER

Your first introduction to the Party Monster will most likely be accompanied by the sound of ice clinking in a glass. This is the sound you'll come to associate with them, as they are always either making a cocktail or shaking an empty glass, ready for another. The Party Monster houseguest will bring their own top-shelf liquor, as they worry about what the host will serve, and be more than willing to share it with other guests. However, if you drink their booze, you have signed an unwritten contract that obligates you to stay up late with them for "just one more." The Party Monster is rarely trouble, as they focus on their buzz, not on what everyone else is doing. The Party Monster is usually a safe bet to hang out with during your stay. Their goal is to simply keep the party going, and they won't draw you into any painful, deep discussions about how yoga changed their life. Though beware that they'll probably give you a nickname; Party Monsters love to give nicknames. Get ready to be called "Captain," "Blondie," or "Cowboy" for the rest of your visit. If tired and feeling the need to escape after multiple nightcaps, offer to get them a drink and make it a bit strong; soon they'll fall asleep and you can tiptoe off to your room.

THE ONE-UPPER

A cousin of the Know-It-All, the One-Upper houseguest claims to have done everything, been everywhere, and know everyone you know; however, their experience and knowledge of anything you mention is far superior to yours. If you say you saw *Book of Mormon*, they've seen it twenty times; if you choose the wine at dinner, they were once a sommelier; if you talk about your trip to Santa Fe, they consider it their second home and once ran for mayor. There is no limit to the lengths they will go to one-up you. One way to deal with this odd behavior is to toy with the One-Upper by creating fake places, events, and even people and seeing whether they will claim to know them. At dinner with your host and other guests, make up the name of a fake restaurant in New York (let's call it the Lava Room) and say you've been dying to go there. Chances are the One-Upper will take the bait and say they've been there. Then, take it a little further and say you forgot where the Lava Room is located in New York. The One-Upper will give a vague response, such as "Over on the East Side." Keep going and Google the Lava Room in front of the One-Upper and appear confused when you can't locate it. The One-Upper will claim it has a secret address given to only a chosen few. Now, go in for the kill: marvel at how well connected the One-Upper is and ask whether they can get you a reservation. They will either bluff and say "No problem" or burst into flames. Either will be fun to watch.

PROFILING HOUSE GUESTS by THEIR LUGGAGE CHOICE

Brings own pillow cases.
Used cotton balls everywhere.
"Your water tastes funny."

Up at dawn to hit outlet malls.

Blows fusebox using hair straightener.

Guest room smells of Bath & Body
Works and Twizzlers.

Here for a Tough Mudder event.

Checks guest room for "bugs".

Takes up half the refrigerator
with cans of Monster energy drink.

In town for EDM festival.
Always shirtless.
Weed dealer in your kitchen.

Blares Fox & Friends.
Asks to borrow hacksaw.
Cat goes missing.

Sleeps on floor next to bed.
Asks about closest OTB.
Definitely using your toothbrush.

GUESTS GONE WILD
Bad Houseguest Behavior

If you break a glass, spill wine on a rug, or do something in the bathroom that requires a plunger, your host will understand. Things like this happen, and you simply apologize and move on. However, there is some horrible houseguest behavior that is impossible to recover from. It will earn you a spot in the Worst Houseguest Hall of Fame and lead your host to say, "They are *NEVER* coming again."

THE FIRST RULE OF HOUSEGUEST

There are very few things most everyone can agree upon, besides that it's impossible not to click on a video of a baby duck making friends with a Labrador retriever and that green peppers ruin everything. It is also universally agreed upon that taking a swing at someone when you're a houseguest is beyond not cool. Physical violence isn't all right at any time, but doing so when you're a guest in someone's home takes it to a whole new level of horrible. If you do something that causes bleeding or the arrival of men in blue with badges, there is no coming back from that. You should head home, where you will hate yourself for eternity.

While physical fighting should send you literally packing, fighting of any sort is to be avoided when you're a houseguest. If you're visiting someone who you know has opinions on certain topics that are very different from yours, check your heated reactions to those opinions at the door. You accepted their invitation knowing how they felt, so while you're in their home, don't bring up topics you know will end with somebody in tears. This extends to your host's other guests too. It's great that you were captain of your college debate team and could destroy their arguments in seconds, but don't do it. A healthy discussion is fine, but don't turn brunch into a *Meet the Press* screaming match. Eat your eggs benedict, smile, and nod and then go watch a baby duck/Labrador video to calm down. Really, it's like video Valium.

MOMMY, I'M SCARED

If you put a scratch on an antique desk, your host won't be happy, but they'll forgive you. If you do anything to upset or remotely endanger your host's children, you are toast. There is no way to recover, and you will be banished forever. Parents are like the Mafia, in that they will never forget or forgive when it comes to their kids. Cross little Jaxton or Sophia and you instantly become persona non grata.

Putting a child in physical danger is, of course, top-tier horrible houseguest behavior. No, it's not all right to take a kid out on a jet ski or let them get up on the roof with you to look at the stars without first asking their parents' permission. Anything with even the tiniest risk factor should first be run by your host, even if the kid says their parents allow them to do it. You are an adult, and they are not, so it's probably a good idea not to trust the judgment of someone wearing a Peppa Pig T-shirt.

Trying to be the "fun" houseguest by letting your host's kids eat things they normally aren't allowed to have is another good way to guarantee the wrath of your host. Giving a kid a second Popsicle might not seem like a big deal to you, but it could cause your host to erupt. Also, lots of kids have food allergies, so, again, always ask your host first. A trip to the emergency room caused by you won't exactly be a good time. And remember that you're the adult, so sneaking your host's underage son or daughter a beer or getting stoned with them is definitely a lame move.

Correcting the behavior of your host's kids is also verboten. Even if their child makes the kid from *The Omen* seem "just a little cranky," it is not your place to discipline them. If you do, you'll be forever remembered as "the person who made our child cry." If their adorable tyke did something really bad, tell the host when the kid isn't around. Be careful how you present it too; make it more "I thought you'd want to know" versus "Your kid is the spawn of Satan."

TWELVE SHEETS TO THE WIND

You're the one who insisted on opening the fifth bottle of wine at dinner. Then you moved on to vodka. Next came the single malt. Then beers . . . several. Nobody could figure out how you found the bottle of tequila the host hid behind the microwave, but you did. Of course, then you wanted to go out and party, so they hid the car keys much better. That didn't stop you, though; you found a bike—a child's bike, pink—that you drove into a tree. Maniacal laughter followed as you raced toward the neighbor's pool while removing your clothes. As your host tried to cajole you into coming inside, you relieved yourself in said pool. Soon, dogs barked, doors slammed, and raised voices came from all directions. You woke the next morning, covered in scratches (no, the cat did **not** want to sleep in your bed), and your head feels like it's in a barbed wire vise. You don't remember much from the previous evening as you stare at the empty peanut butter jar next to the bed and wonder how the door to your room got barricaded with furniture. You know you're going to be sick, but the question is when: do you get it over with now or wait till later so it's almost like a little present you give yourself? *Wait* is your decision as you prepare to get out of bed to face your host downstairs and begin your apology tour. As you drag yourself from the bed, you notice the sheets are damp. Very damp. "Please, let it be water," you pray. "Pleeeeaaaase, let it be water."

WHO'S THAT GUY IN MY SHOWER?

You remember that Brad, from your old job, lives a town over from your host. The Brad-meister was hilarious, and you haven't seen him in a couple

Tolerating Bad Houseguest Behavior
~VS~
How Long you've known Them

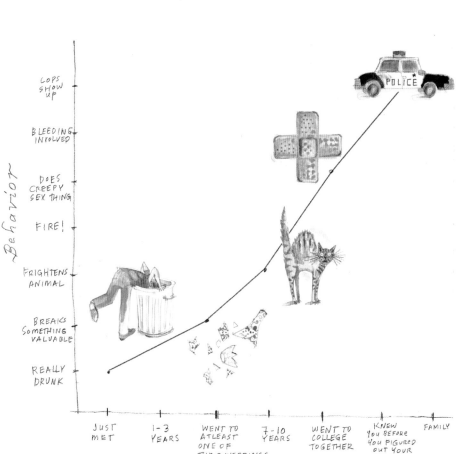

Behavior (y-axis):
- COPS SHOW UP
- BLEEDING INVOLVED
- DOES CREEPY SEX THING
- FIRE!
- FRIGHTENS ANIMAL
- BREAKS SOMETHING VALUABLE
- REALLY DRUNK

Length of Time (x-axis):
- JUST MET
- 1-3 YEARS
- WENT TO ATLEAST ONE OF THEIR WEDDINGS.
- 7-10 YEARS
- WENT TO COLLEGE TOGETHER
- KNEW YOU BEFORE YOU FIGURED OUT YOUR HAIR
- FAMILY

years, so you decide to maybe give that wild man a call and invite him over to your host's place. Put. Down. That. Phone.

Your host invited you, as they wanted to spend time with **you**, not Brad or anyone else you decide to include. It might not seem like such a big deal to invite friends to your host's place, but it could be to your host. It signals that you're not having a good time and that you need to import others for fun. When you bring in new people that only *you* know, it makes things uncomfortable, as you'll have to devote your time talking to that person and your host will feel ignored. Maybe Brad is a great guy and your host will love those SNL characters he does ("Do the Church Lady, Brad!") but introduce them another time.

Also, if you recently started dating someone whom your host has never met, don't bring them along for your visit. Again, your host invited just you, and if you bring someone else, it will mess with the dynamic. It's like when *The Brady Bunch* added Cousin Oliver—it just won't work. Your host will act like an overly polite version of themselves, and your new semi-significant other will feel left out listening to you and your host reminiscing.

Similarly, if you meet someone at bar or start swiping on Tinder while a houseguest, it is not acceptable to invite someone over. You are there to hang out with your host, not to bring a stranger into their home who will make everyone nervous and probably steal your iPad.

THE BLANKET THIEF

—Paul R., Actor, New York

Long before I became an actor, I considered being president of the United States. Right out of college, I took an internship working on Capitol Hill, which I was sure would fast-track me to the White House. This was the 1990s, so most of my time was spent faxing things and hanging out with a lovely fellow intern from Beverly Hills named Monica. I wonder whatever became of her?

I would be in Washington for a month, and I was looking forward to staying in the housing provided for all the interns. I envisioned it as a cross between *The West Wing* and *Animal House*. However, when I arrived, I discovered none of the cool kids stayed in intern housing, as you had to be in by midnight and it was located in Maryland, far from the action on the Potomac.

My parents had old friends, Perry and Lillian (fake names), who had a great house in the heart of Georgetown and graciously offered to host me during my stay. At one point, Perry had been secretary-of-something, a job that garnered him many silver-framed photos of him together with Ronald Reagan. Perry wore ascots and liked gin, both the booze and the card game. Lillian grew orchids and used the word "sublime" a lot. If you think this is about to turn into a *Rosemary's Baby* situation, you're wrong. My hosts were lovely, wonderful people. I'm the one who turned into a horror show houseguest.

The house was pretty big, and I was given my own room with a bathroom on the third floor. It wasn't fancy, but it was far better than the outskirts of Maryland. It was sort of like the butler's quarters at *Downton Abbey*. I was Mr. Bates, but without the limp. Most of my stay was uneventful. I'd occasionally have dinner with Perry and Lillian, but most of the time I was free to come and go as I pleased, and we quietly coexisted. The only other member of the household was Duffy, an excitable, aging schnauzer who plays a pivotal role in this story.

A farewell party for all the interns was planned on the Thursday night prior to our final day of work on Friday. It was held at the Hay-Adams Hotel, and the best thing about it was that it was free. When you're an intern, you live for free things and will go to any event where complimentary food and beverage are a possibility. If there was a speech at the Icelandic embassy on the history of eel fishing that comes with a free buffet, chances are eighty percent of the attendees would be interns.

The intern farewell party was very fun, and I, of course, overdid it in terms of cocktail consumption. I wasn't blind drunk, but I exhibited all the usual signs of someone well past their limit: slurred speech, widespread proclaiming that everyone was my best friend, and the need to eat a giant burrito at 2:00 a.m.

After the burrito, I headed home to bed. At around 4:00 a.m. I woke with a jolt, feeling like my stomach had been placed in one of those machines that shakes paint at Home Depot. Before I could make it to the bathroom, let's just say the cocktails and the burrito came back to visit . . . all over the electric blanket on my bed. Despite feeling terrible, I set out to try to clean the blanket in the middle of the night.

I snuck downstairs to the basement. I considered putting the blanket in the washing machine, but it dawned on me that electric blankets probably don't fare well in washing machines. So I started cleaning it by hand, gagging as I scrubbed it in the sink. As I scrubbed, I felt something pulling on the blanket and looked down to see Duffy, the schnauzer, eating burrito remnants off the blanket. OK, OK, sorry, we can all gag now.

I tried to shoo the dog away, but whenever I did, it started to bark. If I didn't want to wake up my hosts, I had to allow an animal to eat something that was once inside my body. This was truly a *Walking Dead* moment.

Eventually, Duffy got bored and went upstairs, leaving me with a soggy, putrid blanket. Before I did any more damage, I realized I needed to take the blanket out for professional cleaning. However, I couldn't just walk out the front door in the morning carrying it. My hosts might inquire about the large stinky, dripping thing in my arms. So I decided I would throw the blanket outside and retrieve it on my way to work.

My plan was to toss the blanket out the front door behind some bushes, but when I approached the door, my friend Duffy was back, jumping around, excited to go outside. I also realized I didn't have the alarm code and opening the door would set things off. I was suddenly Jason Bourne, with his plan unraveling before his eyes, knowing he had to do something quick before the bomb went off. Or in my case, the alarm clock, as Perry and Lillian would be waking up soon.

I retreated back to my room to devise a new plan to get the blanket out of the house. I considered taking it out of the house in a shopping bag, but the only bag I could find was from Talbots, a women's clothing store. I decided carrying it out in that would create a whole new set of questions in the minds of my hosts.

In the hallway outside my room was the wall box for the alarm system. While not a security expert, from looking at the box, it appeared that the windows in the house were not hooked up to the system. I could toss the blanket out a window and retrieve it on the way to work as previously planned. I was almost positive the windows weren't connected—but what if they were? A few hours ago, I was a happy, drunk intern, scream-singing "Uptown Girl" in a bar, and now I was trapped in my own private *Hurt Locker*.

I gingerly opened the window in my room and, phew, no alarm. Then out the window I tossed the wet, gross blanket, which plopped behind bushes on the side of the house. My plan was working! I was a genius! Now all I had to do was deal with a blistering hangover and take the blanket to the dry cleaner.

As I rode the bus to my final day of work, nobody suspected the respectable young man carrying a Talbots bag (I folded it in my coat pocket) was in the midst of executing a dastardly plan. I was just another guy in a tie on his way to Capitol Hill who happened to be carrying a disgusting electric blanket covered in several Heinekens, a few shots of Jägermeister, a couple gin and tonics, and a semi-digested burrito.

When I dropped the blanket off at the dry cleaners, the clerk didn't give it a second look. I guess dry cleaners have seen it all, much like emergency room doctors and *Real Housewives* producers. I was to pick it up at the end of the day.

My last day at work was spent saying my goodbyes and nursing my hangover. I highly recommend two full-strength Cokes (no Diet!) and a Big Mac to all those who over-imbibe. Now I just had to pick up the blanket at the cleaners, put it back on my bed, and then head to the train station to go back to New York.

I arrived at the dry cleaner right before closing. My blanket was hanging behind the counter, looking all fresh and new in its plastic bag. Hello, clean friend! The clerk brought the blanket to the counter and then said something that still makes me shudder: "Fifty-two fifty." My stomach flipped, and my ears began to ring. How could it possibly cost that much to clean a blanket? He began to explain, but I heard only occasional words like "electrical system," "specialist," and "rush order." I had only sixty bucks to my name, and I still had to buy a train ticket home. I knew decisions had to be made. Should I pay the dry cleaner and somehow find another way home, or do I wave goodbye to the blanket knowing that Lillian and Perry will forever wonder whether their friend's son was some freakish bedding thief?

It's painful to even type, but I proved myself to be a horrible houseguest and went with the latter. I left the electric blanket at the dry cleaner and walked away. I knew it was wrong, my parents would know it was wrong, and, yes, even Duffy would know it was wrong.

It feels good to finally unburden myself after all these years by admitting to this story. I figured if I ever do consider being president again, it would no doubt come out anyway.

IF THE AIR MATTRESS
IS A-ROCKIN'
Sex and the Houseguest

As Salt-N-Pepa once funktastically encouraged us to do: let's talk about sex. As a houseguest, your sex life shouldn't be high on your list of priorities. Your host has provided you a bed, and that bed should be reserved for sleeping, channel surfing, and irrational worrying, just like it is at home. Besides, you're usually a houseguest for only a few days, so if you can't handle a brief period of abstinence, maybe look into one of those clinics that congressmen check into when they get caught sending photos to interns.

If you're a houseguest for a longer period of time (ten-days plus), it's understandable you might have needs of the primal variety. However, you should consider the overall situation you're in before you decide to get busy. If you're staying with family, the answer to whether you have sex is a flat-out ABSOLUTELY NOT. Family members have zero boundaries and would have no problem barging into your room to get the "good scissors" while you're attempting to do that thing you read about on Reddit. If a parent walked in on you, the therapy bills would be staggering, and shudder to think if a sibling (or, worse, an in-law) caught you in the act when you're a houseguest in their home. They would lord it over you forever, exaggerating and elaborating the facts so that what they witnessed sounds so vile you'd assume they had to torch the bed and board up the guest room like post-meltdown Chernobyl. To avoid soul-crushing humiliation, it's probably best to wait till you're back home before getting frisky.

If you're staying with friends who have a more relaxed attitude, sex is permissible, but again, weigh the situation. If your host just announced they're getting divorced, lost their job, or recently threw Grandpa's ashes in the ocean, be respectful and postpone plans to get your freak on.

Also, if your host has kids, remember that kids love to ask questions and run into rooms unannounced. You don't want to be the one who forced your host into having a premature conversation with little Harper, explaining why the visitor people were playing a really weird game of piggyback.

When and if the circumstances do allow for sex, discretion is everything. It should happen *only* in a bed—no terrace, shower, or hot tub hijinks; you are not Machine Gun Kelly. Always try to be quiet and plan it when others aren't around or are asleep. You are allowed to have sex *only* with the person you arrived with—no bringing random strangers you meet online or at a bar into your host's home. Don't bring any "toys" with you either; you're there to visit your host, not explore boundaries, so leave any latex or battery-operated friends at home. Their dog would no doubt find them and turn them into chew toys, taking your level of embarrassment to new heights. Also remember to get rid of all evidence; toss your sheets in the laundry and look under the bed, because there's always something under the bed. These rules also apply to sex of the solo variety. If you decide to give yourself a self-guided pleasure tour, be as discreet as you would be if another party was involved. Do nothing that would cause your host to say, "Is someone being tortured in there?"

If something catastrophic should happen while you're engaged in some horizontal entertainment, like breaking the bed or ruining the linens, first ask yourself what you're doing with your life. Then own up to it and tell your host. It's much better to tell them yourself than having them discover something weird after you leave.

Sex with your host or anyone else who's also staying in your host's home is also an absolute NO. Can you imagine eating pancakes the next morning with everyone in the house knowing exactly what transpired the night before? OK, not everyone—there will always be one clueless person who keeps asking why everyone is being "so quiet."

CHARLESTON LESSONS

—Bill T., Reading, Pennsylvania

A honeymoon in Provence is something my wife, Lisa, and I had always dreamed about. We wanted to walk in fields of lavender, eat cheese with names we couldn't pronounce, and befriend a donkey named Maurice. However, our long-planned honeymoon to France was scheduled to begin the first week of September 2001, a very sad week in history when most things came to a halt, including all air travel. Even though we couldn't fly, we thought it was important to try to have some semblance of a honeymoon, so we scrambled to figure out a plan. One of my college roommates, Kirk, who lived in Boston, graciously offered to let us use his vacation home in Charleston, South Carolina, for a week. Neither Lisa nor I had ever been to Charleston, and after doing a brief internet dive, we were sold. Cobblestone streets, amazing restaurants, beautiful architecture . . . there might even be a friendly donkey!

Our drive down went smoothly; however, upon arriving in Charleston, finding Kirk's house proved a little tricky. A lot of the historic homes looked alike, and his carriage house was tucked behind another home, so there was no address to look for. We eventually located the keys under a flower pot as Kirk had instructed and let ourselves in. The house had a very minimal design aesthetic with subtle shades of gray and blue and eggshell everything. It had a very soothing, peaceful vibe. If the makers of Valium ever got into interior decorating, this would be their showhouse. Kirk had really undersold the place to me, calling it "just a nice, quiet little place not far from the beach." This place was gorgeous. I remarked to Lisa that Kirk had definitely upped his decorating game since college, when his only pieces of furniture were a red couch in the shape of lips and a Coleman cooler used as a coffee table.

I texted Kirk to say that everything was fine, and he told us to make ourselves at home, so we settled in to the master suite. The room did not disappoint. There was a four-poster canopy bed, a large bathroom with a sauna shower, and a small deck that overlooked a garden. I thought Kirk mentioned there was a koi pond, but I didn't see it. We decided that maybe the koi went away to koi camp or were taking their kids back to college. We were beyond thrilled with our digs and would not be writing "Outraged by the lack of orange Japanese fish!" in the guestbook. We spent our first few days discovering all the great things about Charleston. The whole town felt like we were in a storybook with its perfect weather, horse-drawn carriages, and rainbow-colored houses. As we strolled down the Battery and looked out over the ocean, we both agreed that maybe a Provence honeymoon was a little overrated.

"Did you notice there aren't any family photos in the house?" asked my rather observant wife. I of course had not, but I told Lisa I attributed the lack of photos to the fact Kirk that had recently gone through a messy divorce, so maybe he didn't want any reminders, a whole "clean slate" kind of thing. I got a half nod from Lisa on my conclusion, as she decided lots of photos of people with sweaters tied around their necks wouldn't work within the minimalist Zen decor anyhow. Either way, it was just fewer things for us to knock off tables and possibly break.

One day on our way home from several hours of shopping and eating (two of our three favorite honeymoon activities), we ran into an attractive older woman walking a small, adorable dog down our street. Her steel gray hair was pulled into a tight bun, and both she and her dog were wearing matching plaid raincoats. There was no possible way Lisa wasn't going to stop and chat her up. "Your dog is ador—" "Dandie Dinmont," the woman said, interrupting Lisa. "The breed. Everyone asks," she added.

We learned the woman's name was Violet, she'd lived in Charleston her entire life, and she didn't suffer fools. Violet was a rather formidable woman who spoke in headlines, with a slight military cadence. "Widow eight years . . . aneurysm, boom, gone," she said. Violet told us her late husband had been a rear admiral in the navy, which might explain her very stern "here are the facts" manner of speaking. Violet seemed to know everything about everyone in the neighborhood, whether they wanted her to know or not. "We're staying right over there at my friend Kirk's," I said, pointing toward the carriage house. "Divorced. Boston banker," said Violet's latest news update.

"The place is lovely. It's actually our honeymoon," volunteered Lisa. "Congratulations. Small for a honeymoon," replied Violet. I wasn't sure what she meant; Kirk's place was more than large enough for two people, and to us it was perfect for a romantic getaway. I assumed Violet had very high standards; I mean, she and her dog were both wearing Burberry trench coats. "Oh, it's fine for us, and we're out in the garden most of the time anyhow," said Lisa. "Garden?" Violet said, sounding mildly annoyed. "There's no garden," she said. I half expected her to add, "You foolish couple." Lisa and I paused and looked at each other, knowing that contradicting Violet would be pointless. "Nap time," Violet said, nodding toward her dog, and off they went. There would be no goodbye, no enjoy your stay; Violet had a schedule, damn it, and it was time to go. "She never told us the dog's name," Lisa said wistfully. "I'm guessing Patton," I said.

Our honeymoon was turning out exactly as we hoped it would. We had no real plans, no list of things we needed to see; every day we just rolled out of bed (late, wink) and then went with the flow of things. Ever since meeting our plaid-coated neighbor and pooch, we joked whether various things would be "Violet approved." Cab driver who took shortcuts: Violet approved. Restaurant that took forty minutes to bring entrees: NOT Violet approved. All in all, Charleston was proving to be all you could ask for in a honeymoon location.

The house phone in the carriage house had rung a few times during our stay; however, we never answered it, as we assumed if Kirk needed to reach us, he'd call my cell phone. The day before we were to leave, the house phone rang very early in the morning, and I groggily answered it from the bedside table. "Hello," I said. "Who is this?" barked the voice on the other end. "Um, this is Bill," I said, surprised someone was already angry at 6:00 a.m. "What are you doing there? How did you get in?" the voice said, getting louder and meaner. "I'm a friend of Kirk. He's letting us stay here. Who is this, please?" I said, starting to get annoyed. "Kirk who? And WHO is US?" said mean phone person. "Kirk is a very good friend of mine. He's out of town, and he's letting my wife and I stay at his house. We're on our honeymoon," I said, hoping to clear things up and go back to sleep. "Why the hell would my neighbor Kirk tell you to stay at MY house? I don't know what you're up to, pal, but the cops are on their way," he said, sounding dead serious. Lisa could hear the loud voice on the other end of the phone and sat up in bed. "What's going on? Who are you talking to?" she said. "Honeymoon? In MY clean bed?" the mean voice said, now sounding like he'd had the wind knocked out of him. "I'm in Kirk's house!" I said. "You know Kirk, right?" "Yes, but if you're answering MY phone, then you're in MY house," he said, trying to push his rage genie back in the bottle. "Kirk's house is BEHIND my house." At that moment, a montage flashed in my brain, and everything started to make sense. The hard-to-find address. The surprisingly minimal decor. The lack of family photos. Violet's insistence there was no garden. The missing koi pond. I then turned to Lisa and said, "Holy shit. We've been staying in the wrong house."

After a series of calls between Kirk, myself, and his neighbor (who was named Sam and actually a very nice guy), we managed to piece together what happened. Both Kirk and Sam had carriage houses behind the main house; however, Kirk's was about three hundred yards beyond Sam's and hidden by some foliage from Sam's garden (see, there WAS a garden,

Violet!). Both Kirk and Sam also employed the same very high-tech security system of spare key under a flower pot, so when we found the key under Sam's pot, we looked no further. One of Sam's neighbors saw lights on in his place, so they texted him to see why he was in town. Luckily for us, Kirk and Sam were good friends, so he understood the mix-up, and all talk of the police and zip-tie handcuffs went away. We of course apologized profusely and offered to pay Sam for our time at his place. He declined and joked he'd just randomly send friends to stay at Kirk's house sometime to make up for it. We did buy him a new set of sheets (high thread count!) as a gift and paid to have his place cleaned after we left.

We moved to Kirk's house for our last night in Charleston so that the cleaners could get in early to Sam's place and do a thorough "imagine this was a crime scene" cleaning. Kirk's house was exactly as he had described, and we made sure we recognized at least a couple people in the family photos before we settled in. I think we would have had just as good a time if we had stayed in Kirk's *actual* place the entire time. Yes, the shower sauna at Sam's was pretty awesome, but, hey, now we had a koi pond. One of the koi seemed to be in charge and bossed the other fish around. We named her Violet.

ANIMALS, CHILDREN, AND HOUSEGUESTS, OH MY
Dealing with Pets and Kids

When you're a houseguest, you might forget that in addition to your host, there are other residents of the home of the shorter and the four-legged variety. (Most) kids and (most) pets are great fun, and your host will be thrilled when you show that you're a fan of these creatures that they love a hell of a lot more than you. It doesn't matter whether you actually like children and pets; when you're a houseguest, you must at least pretend to like them and do a really convincing job of it. These Lego-loving juice box junkies and furry sofa sleepers aren't going anywhere. You're invading their turf, and they won't be shy about letting you know it. It's up to you to prove to your host that you enjoy their kids, cats, and dogs just as much as they do. Though, if they own a ferret, don't bother; pretending to like one is next to impossible.

One sure way to get on the good side of your host's kids is bribery. When you arrive, always bring your host's kids something. It doesn't need to be expensive, but it should be something they probably don't already have and be a little quirky. Books and clothes are great for birthdays, but a kid will think you're way cooler if you arrive with an ant farm or a Magic 8 Ball. Your present is also a way for you to connect with the kid that doesn't seem forced. These mini–Holden Caulfields know a phony from a mile away and will dismiss you quickly if they sense you're just trying to get on their good side to impress their parents. Speak to them normally; don't talk down to them or use some strange "I'm talking to a child" voice. Ask kids questions and have an actual conversation. Your host will get a full report on you from their kids, so don't blow it.

You may not be used to having kids around, so be aware you may have to change your behavior a little. Don't swear around the kids. Kids love to repeat things, and if they hear you say *a bad word*, chances are your host's kid will be repeating it in about point three seconds, so watch your language when the kids are nearby. Also, no telling of dirty jokes or letting kids watch something you know their parents wouldn't approve of. That would be considered creepy.

You can't get around the fact that some kids are just brats. It's hard to sit there and smile as a preschooler kicks you in the shins or pulls the cat's tail, but when you're a houseguest, disciplining your host's kids is **not** your job. Sure, if you find them with matches and a can of gasoline, you can step in, but in most cases if a host's kid is being a nightmare, leave the correcting to them. Good hosts will quickly put the kibosh on bratty behavior. However, if the host doesn't tell their kid to knock it off, ignore them or retreat to your room. You are a houseguest, and your advice on how to deal with the situation will not be welcomed no matter how well intended. Though once back in your room, feel free to mutter, "That three-year-old is an asshole."

Deciding whether to bring your own children along when you're a houseguest is something to seriously consider. Even if your host says to pack up your sippy cups and come over, a voice in your head tells you they secretly hope you'll leave them home with Gramma. If you do decide to bring your kids, you must be prepared to continue parenting duties during your stay. Don't think you can show up at your host's place, hand your kid an iPad, then start doing Jell-O shots and scoop them up when you leave.

Also, before your trip, do some serious prep work with your kids, making it clear that they must to be on their best behavior. Whatever tactic you need to use to guarantee a tantrum-free visit is allowed. Vague hints about a Disney World trip, threats of telling Santa, a half promise to let them get their ears pierced—whatever you have to say to get them to toe the line is allowed. If the host has children, make sure that your kids understand they're expected to be extra, extra nice to them. There will be sharing, there will be good sportsmanship, there will be no blood. If it turns out that your kids and your host's kids hate each other, it's better to make up an excuse and leave early. If you stay, nobody will have any fun, and you'll run the risk of some horrible scene that will be whispered about at peewee soccer games for years to come.

Some people are cat people, some people are dog people, and some people have no souls and dislike both. When you're a houseguest, it doesn't really matter where you stand; you have to appear to love all creatures great and small and slobbering. Upon arriving at your host's place, you'll no doubt be greeted by their dog. This moment is crucial, as your host will be watching to see how you react. A good host will be aware that a furry thing with teeth running toward anyone can be unnerving and will make sure they have control of the animal till it's used to someone new in the house. Showing a degree of trepidation when first encountering a dog is fine; however, cowering in the corner screaming, "Get that thing away from me!" will not start things off on the right foot. Most dogs are excited to meet someone new who might toss them part of a morning bagel and will soon become your friend. During your stay, if your host talks exclusively in baby talk to their dogs and dresses them in little outfits, go with it. Yes, they view their dogs as their children, but as long as they don't start looking at preschools for them, it's really not hurting anyone. If your host owns a cat, it will probably spend most of the time hiding from you or silently judging you. If it decides to jump on your lap, give it a second before pushing it off; you might actually like it. If the cat starts using your thigh as a scratching post, you can remove it from your lap, but do it in a way that doesn't draw attention. If you're allergic to cats, you need to decide whether you want to spend your visit sneezing and popping Claritin or just stay home.

THEY DON'T WANT ANOTHER CANDLE
The Houseguest Gift

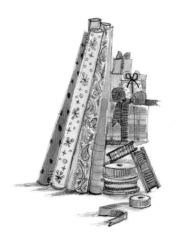

Like everyone else, you no doubt remember exactly where you were when you heard the news. Gwyneth Paltrow created a candle that smells like a vagina, but not just any vagina, *her* vagina. Yup, for seventy-five dollars you could buy a Goop candle called "This Smells Like My Vagina." Candles have become the go-to houseguest gift. Though a nice little token, they kind of signal you didn't exactly rack your brain when deciding what to buy . . . but you knew you had to get them *something*. There are some great candles out there, but how do you know whether your host wants their home to smell like grapefruit-vanilla, a Greek Orthodox church, or lady parts? Unless you know your host's taste incredibly well, you might want to explore some other options.

Your choice of a houseguest gift should go hand in hand with how well you know the host. People you know really well don't expect you to go crazy and show up with a Hermès blanket, but they will appreciate something you knew they'd actually like, even if it didn't cost a lot. That weird brand of Italian toothpaste they use, five pints of that limited-batch Ben & Jerry's they love—things like this are great, as they show you actually *thought* about the gift. However, choose wisely, because giving a lame houseguest gift to someone you know *really* well will haunt you for eternity. It will become a running joke, and they'll pull it out to show others whenever you're around. "Hey, have you seen the Princess Leia soap dispenser that Mark gave us? The soap comes out of her buns." You'll try to defend your gift to no avail, exclaiming, "But you love Carrie Fisher!"

Anything that can be construed as a gag gift should be avoided. Gag gifts as a whole are pointless. Why not just set fire to fifteen dollars instead of buying that Dane Cook quote toilet paper? Wine is always a strong option, as you probably know what close friends like to drink, but it better be good. Good meaning it should cost at least twenty-five bucks a bottle. People Google—they just do.

If your host isn't a close friend, you have a bit more leeway. Your goal here is to make whatever gift you give look as expensive as possible. Handing someone a jar of honey won't elicit any squeals of delight, but put that sucker in a plaid gift bag with tissue paper and tie the handles with a satin ribbon—boom, you're golden. Also, the store packaging your gift came in is probably cheesy, so take it out of the bad packaging and put whatever you bought in a nice box, but **not** a box from a fancy store you have lying around. You are fooling nobody, and the mere thought of your host trying to return your Target pepper grinder at Tiffany should give you chills. The Container Store is a good resource for boxes and most every-thing else to upgrade your gift. And take off the damn price tags. Sheesh.

Regifting is allowed, but only if you genuinely think your host will like something that you didn't want. However, it cannot be **used**; it has to be in the same condition it was when you received it. Sorry, it doesn't matter if you used only a tiny teaspoon of that imported olive oil or barely cracked the binding of that coffee-table book about Japanese tea houses; those items are considered used and off limits as gifts. A big rookie regifting mistake is failing to check the box you were given for any gift cards or errant pieces of wrapping paper or tape; these telltale signs will instantly expose you and forever brand you as a regifter, so make sure to check for any evidence.

There's no rule that says you have to arrive with a house gift. Sometimes it's better to send a gift after your stay, as you may have noticed your host needed something while you were visiting. They might be low on wine glasses or could use new beach towels, or maybe at dinner one night they said, "You know what—I really wish our house smelled like a vagina." If that should happen, you know exactly what to get them.

NOTABLE MOMENTS
in Fancy Candle History

200 B.C.
China makes candles from whale fat. Chinese whales go into hiding.

1500
Catholic church switches to beeswax candles as Popes realize value of good lighting.

1879
Lightbulb invented. Whales and bees relax.

1961
Diptyque opens first shop in Paris. misspelling of Diptyque begins.

1963
Jo Malone is born. England soon to smell like more than chip shops and stale ale.

1993
Scented soy candles introduced, bringing about universal vegan smugness.

2018
Tom Ford creates candle called "Fucking Fabulous." Fucking fabulous people everywhere rejoice.

2019
J.Lo orders fifty Le Labo Santal candles per month.

2020
GOOP releases "This Smells Like My Vagina" Candle. Chris Martin, Brad Pitt, Ben Affleck get unusually high amount of text messages.

COMMON TRAITS

— OF —
HOUSEGUESTS, TERMITES &
FASCIST DICTATORS

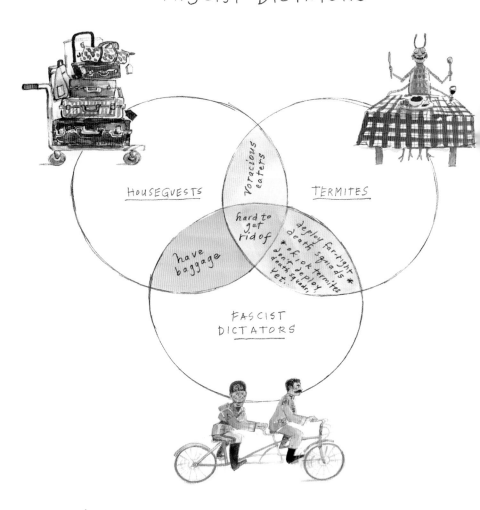

HOUSEGUESTS

TERMITES

FASCIST DICTATORS

voracious eaters

hard to get rid of

have baggage

deploy far-right death squads *

* 610k termites don't deploy death squads, yet.

CHAPTER 17

SO LONG, FAREWELL, AUF WIEDERSEHEN ... GET THE HELL OUT

Whenever the topic of houseguests is brought up, people invariably mention the quote about fish and houseguests smelling after three days. They can't help it; it's this involuntary reaction like yawning after someone else yawns or hearing the name Austin Powers and not saying "Yeah, baby." Whether this quote attributed to Ben Franklin (but what isn't?) is accurate or not is debatable. Some houseguests you want gone after they've been in your home about ten minutes, while other guests you're happy to host indefinitely. Usually, a houseguest and host mutually understand when it's time to leave. However, there are times when a houseguest doesn't take the hint and the host must do a little nudging to get them out the door.

If your host says things like "Too bad you won't *be here* then" or "Oh, that's happening long after *you're gone*," take that as a sign that it's getting close to departure time. If subtlety doesn't work, they might write your name on a kitchen calendar and circle the date or start talking about redecorating the guest room *once you leave*, taking window measurements and asking your opinion on paint samples: "Do you think our guest coming *after you* would like 'Mole's Breath' or 'November Mourn'?"

When it is time to leave, you want to do all you can to stay in the good graces of your host. It doesn't require a lot of effort to do some things that will make your host glad they had you in their home.

THE GUEST BOOK

Some hosts like to have their guests sign a guest book. No, it's not a clever way to get a sample of your handwriting to send to Quantico for analysis. Hosts use the book as a little history of their home and a fun way to remember guests. This practice has become more common due to Pinterest and Etsy, two businesses that have flourished by encouraging people to post and purchase all things adorable related to home entertainment. Guest book popularity is right up there with kitchen chalkboards and signs made out of twigs that say "Blessed."

When signing the guest book, hosts aren't expecting you to be overly clever or quippy. There's no need to try to be the new Dorothy Parker and "win" with your hilarious comment. Your name, hometown, and date of visit is more than enough. If you do have something to say about your stay, keep it brief. Nobody likes a page hog who rambles on and on. If your handwriting is large or unruly, try to rein it in, keeping your message on par in size with previous guests' entries on the page, so as not to ruin the aesthetics of the book. This might seem like overthinking things, but do you really want to be known forever as the guest who wrote in Zodiac Killer bold?

While a positive comment is appreciated, your host does NOT want to hear your thoughts on what they could improve or do better. This is the guest book, not a suggestion box, so no "Might be time for a new mattress" or "Too bad there wasn't any soy milk."

YOUR ROOM

Leave no trace. This maxim popularized by all those with carabiner key chains encourages people to be responsible and leave as small an imprint as possible when in the wilderness. This great outdoors rallying cry is also applicable to guest rooms, as you should make sure that your room doesn't look like the aftermath of an EDM festival after you leave. When you're a houseguest, leaving no trace means making an effort to leave your room in a state that's close to the way it was when you arrived. Clear the room of any dirty dishes, strip the bed linens, and gather the wet towels. Check with your host as to where they'd like you to put them; usually it's near the laundry room, but best to ask in case they have a preference. Throw out any trash and wipe down the bathroom—you don't have to scrub everything, but at least make sure things are presentable. Open a window, too, as airing the room out will be appreciated. When your host opens the guest room door after you leave, you want them to be surprised by what they see . . . in a good way.

LUGGAGE

You might not realize it, but luggage gets dirty when dragging it through airports and tossing it in car trunks. So when packing, don't put your bag on the bed or, if you do, make sure to put a towel down first. This will eliminate any mysterious skid marks on the bedding after you're gone.

If you can't carry your bag up and down a flight of stairs without pulling a muscle and need help from your host in order to zip it, probably rethink what you've packed. You don't want to have to mumble apologies to your host as they struggle to help you carry it.

Also, don't leave any luggage behind and plan to pick it up later. A couple of days is fine, but your host's home is not a storage unit. If you leave luggage at your host's, don't act surprised if it's damaged or somehow your underwear ends up in a garage sale.

TRANSPORTATION

Get your own. Your host may offer to drive you to the airport or train station, but they are hoping you refuse, so you should. Hosting someone in your home is incredibly generous, so don't push things by assuming your host will be your chauffeur as well. Also, look into how long it takes to get to where you're headed long before you leave. Your host is not Google Maps, either, nor do they have encyclopedic knowledge of flights and train schedules, so do some research.

Even though your host sincerely enjoyed having you stay, they will also sincerely enjoy having you leave. If you say you're leaving at three, *leave at three*; don't dawdle or hang around. Your host wants their house back so they can relax and go back to their routine. Pack up your car, call an Uber, or start pulling your wheely luggage (that you still wish you got in a different color) out the door—it's time to go.

THE GOODBYE

The actual goodbye is more important than you think. Hosts seem to remember the goodbye and how it was executed. If your host is not going to be home when you head out, make sure to say goodbye before they leave. No, a note is not just as good; the face-to-face farewell is always the way to go. Besides, you'll get to find out whether your host is a hugger or not. Some are, some aren't, and if you happen to be high on the hugging spectrum, don't force a hug on your host if you sense they are hug averse.

If there are other people living in the home where you stayed, make an effort to say goodbye to them as well. It's much easier to stick your head in a room and say "Bye, great seeing you!" than later hearing that your host's kids were sad you didn't say goodbye to them. (Remember: do **not** make children sad; see: "Animals, Children, and Houseguests, Oh My").

SUBTEXT OF THE GUEST BOOK

Thanks for the lively 4th of July

Your kids are brats

I'LL NEVER FORGET YOUR MEMORABLE GUEST ROOM!

You've got mice

what an eclectic group of friends!

Your neighbors asked me to do a three-way

PLAYLIST FOR HOUSEGUESTS WHO'VE OVERSTAYED THEIR WELCOME

"Too Good at Goodbyes"
—Sam Smith

"Midnight Train to Georgia"
—Gladys Knight and the Pips

"Leaving on a Jet Plane"
—John Denver

"Shut Up and Drive"
—Rihanna

"Fast Car"
—Tracy Chapman

"Homeward Bound"
—Simon and Garfunkel

"Before You Go"
—Lewis Capaldi

"Bye Bye Bye"
—*NSYNC

"Time for Me to Fly"
—REO Speedwagon

"Waving through a Window"
—*Dear Evan Hansen*, cast album

ACKNOWLEDGMENTS

Thanks to everyone who hosted me while I wrote this book and to all those who tolerated listening to me talk about it. VIP Platinum Status thanks to Dana, Mark, Wilson, and Maddie Strong; Susan and Sten Sandlund; Janet Currie and Donald Dudley; Robin Saunders and Ella and Savannah; Adam Higginbotham and Vanessa Mobley; Shrevie and Jim Shepherd; and Spencer Carbone.

Triple Miles with Extra Legroom thanks to Emilio Nunez, Eric Ajemian, Beth and Ken Kurtz, Matt and Jessica Enstice, Emily and Beau Barron, Shasca and Zen Martinoli, Gigi Gatewood and Anders Johnson, George Varino, Brent Stoller, David Morgan, Fred Spencer, Amy Corcoran and Charles Spiegel, David Shafei, John and Mia Coveny, Jerry Jensen, Andy Green, Ted McCagg, Ahmer Kalam, Marianne Raphael and Conner Williams, Jim Jung, Sid Karger and Jean Michel Placent, Larry Burnett, Paula Enstice, Anthony Enstice, Axel Dupeaux, Theo Blackston, Lisa Baker, and Brian Bremner.

Special Early Boarding thanks to Joanie Hall for the title and Bob Hall for always picking up lunch.

Thanks to my ever-optimistic agent, Monika Verma, who sat beside me on the traveling-carnival, rickety-roller-coaster ride of this book. Thanks to my editor, Betty Wong, for her guidance and never yelling at me.

© Mark Strong

ABOUT THE AUTHOR

Tom Coleman is an Emmy-nominated writer and filmmaker who has worked with MTV, *Esquire*, and *McSweeney's*. He is the author of *I Actually Wore This: Clothes We Can't Believe We Bought* (Rizzoli). Tom has the haircut of a lesser-known nineteenth-century vice president and may very well be staying in your guest room right now. Write him at guestiquettethebook@gmail.com.

ABOUT THE ILLUSTRATOR

Illustrator and Creative Director Joe Stuart is celebrated for his whimsical design sense, attention to detail, and impressive collection of plaid shirts. He has won numerous awards including three Emmys. Joe lives in Chicago with his wife, two kids, and three dogs—all of whom agree that Wes Anderson really needs to try another typeface besides Futura.